Advance Praise

"The *Flourish* series will never, ever leave the top of my desk; it is a comprehensive guide for life. Its insight and organization are amazing. I don't know how one person could compose the whole world of what is right. I am looking forward to following the path of this masterpiece."

—**Dr. Story Musgrave**, surgeon, Marine veteran,
six-time NASA astronaut and Hubble Space Telescope repairman,
Kissimmee, Florida

"I am absolutely blown away by Mark's fact-based analysis and suggested remedies on such a huge scale. A tremendous series and worthy of careful reading."

—**Paul de Lima**, former CEO and owner of Paul de Lima Coffee,
Syracuse, New York

"A magnum opus? Is it bold, monumental, brilliant, provocative, impossible, or outrageous? It's all of this and more. Bitz insightfully nails how America has lost its way. Then he ventures forth with thoughtful and sometimes radical solutions about how to find our way back. A courageous and important series."

—**Bob Vanourek**, award-winning author and former CEO of five firms, Cordillera, Colorado

"The *Flourish* series provides a roadmap for living a healthy, useful, and happy life... mandatory reading for every high school student...

—**Mi**... former CEO and owner of Road Machinery and Supplies, Duluth, Minnesota

"Mark has written clearly and truthfully, a complete operator's manual for life. I will share the series with those who are dearest to me."

—**Haisook Somers**, mother, award-winning maple syrup producer, philanthropist, and volunteer, Montreal, Quebec

"I am profoundly impressed with the *Flourish* series. Mark has delineated and backed up with facts and thoughtful analysis timeless truths and behaviors that will help many individuals lead more fulfilled lives. His work could not come at a better time. As fewer people learn these truths and behaviors from their families and faiths, an insightful, well-organized, secular expression of them becomes ever more important."

—**John Doyle**, Owner and CEO of Doyle Security Systems, Rochester, New York

"Mark blends his considerable experience to design a plan for America to not only grow but also to flourish. His practical and common sense plan is a must read for all thinking Americans."

—**Carl Youngman**, former CEO of more than twenty companies, Boston, Massachusetts

"Mark delves into some of our country's biggest challenges and cuts through the politics. He takes you beyond the approaches of the right and left and presents creative and practical winning ones."

—**Stephen McConnell**, president of Solano Ventures, Scottsdale, Arizona

"I find myself staring off into space and pondering Mark's ideas. I agree with what he says, and I am pleased to find so much well-synthesized and organized thought in one treatise."

—**Tom Ewert,** retired federal judge, Naples, Florida

"The *Flourish* series is thought-provoking and thoroughly interesting. It examines many of our country's challenges and offers a comprehensive set of solutions. It is incredibly innovative and has stimulated many discussions among our family and friends. The books are a must read for the leaders of our country and those who are concerned about it."

—**Mark Danni,** artistic director, Theatre Zone, and president of Karemar Productions, Naples, Florida

"Wow! The *Flourish* series is comprehensive and very thought-provoking. It will encourage many a vigorous debate around the kitchen table."

—**Carole-Ann Miller**, CEO, Camsa, Inc., Halifax, Canada

"Mark's series should be mandatory reading for all sixteen- to twenty-two-year-old students. It would work well in a Western Civics and a Future Civilization course."

—**Gary Fenchuk,** real estate developer, Midlothian, Virginia

"Even though I have a more biblical viewpoint of the world, the teaching and wisdom of *Flourish* should be mandatory reading for all first-year college students."

—**Kenneth Lockard**, founder of numerous companies, CEO of Lockard Companies, Cedar Falls, Iowa

"Every chapter is worth reading and pondering."

—**Richard Kaufman,** chair of Amstore Corporation, Chicago, Illinois

FLOURISH

Toward Truth, Freedom, Fitness, and Decency

MARK W. BITZ

GREENLEAF
BOOK GROUP PRESS

This publication is designed to provide accurate and authoritative information in regard to the subject matter covered. It is sold with the understanding that the publisher and author are not engaged in rendering legal, accounting, or other professional services. If legal advice or other expert assistance is required, the services of a competent professional should be sought.

Published by Greenleaf Book Group Press
Austin, Texas
www.gbgpress.com

Distributed by Greenleaf Book Group

For ordering information or special discounts for bulk purchases, please contact Greenleaf Book Group at PO Box 91869, Austin, TX 78709, 512.891.6100.

Design and composition by Greenleaf Book Group
Cover design by Greenleaf Book Group
Cover image: ©iStockphoto.com/pro_

Cataloging-in-Publication data is available.

Print ISBN: 978-1-62634-435-8

eBook ISBN: 978-1-62634-436-5

Part of the Tree Neutral® program, which offsets the number of trees consumed in the production and printing of this book by taking proactive steps, such as planting trees in direct proportion to the number of trees used: www.treeneutral.com

TreeNeutral®

Printed in the United States of America on acid-free paper

17 18 19 20 21 22   10 9 8 7 6 5 4 3 2 1

First Edition

So you and future generations may realize
your full potential and do better than we have done.

Contents

List of Figures

Introduction

Good intentions, idyllic wishes, and flawed policies do not improve people's lives.

Like so many other Americans, I am a product of people who came to this country in search of a better life. Three of my grandparents were of Anglo-Saxon and one was of German descent. My Anglo-Saxon ancestors came to America in the seventeenth and eighteenth centuries, and my German ancestors in the nineteenth century. And like so many other Americans, life improved for each generation of my ancestors throughout our country's history. Sadly, this is not to be the case for the current generation, as our nation no longer exhibits the vitality and the promise that it did in prior decades.

Many American children live with one parent and grow up in poverty. Many do not receive a good education. Healthcare costs, social welfare costs, and government debt escalate. Good-paying jobs flee the country. Millions of illegal aliens enter the country. Immigrant assimilation is no longer a priority, and a common language and culture no longer unify us. Inequality increases. Social mobility declines. People struggle to maintain the living standard that they achieved years ago.

Radical Islam and terrorist threats grow. China and Russia expand their geographic influence and footprint. Natural ecosystems degrade, and billions of tons of climate-altering carbon dioxide spew into the atmosphere each year. Polarizing politics, laws, policies, news, and speech separate us. Dysfunctional federal and state governments fail us. Why are our challenges mounting, and why are we no longer ascending?

In 1978, at age nineteen, I participated in a field study through Guatemala, Costa Rica, Honduras, and Colombia. A year later, I participated in another one through Western Europe, Eastern Europe, and the former Soviet Union. The contrasts between life in Upstate New York and many of these countries shocked me. The experiences started me thinking about what causes some people to prosper and others to subsist.

Although there are many causes of individual and national prosperity, I recognized at an early age that the overarching one is culture.

> **Culture** is human software that orchestrates our activity. It is the perspectives, practices, and taboos that parents, teachers, and others transmit to us, and the art, heroes, and achievements that groups celebrate to reinforce the transmission.

International economic and cultural differences are not the only ones that I experienced during my college years. Soon after entering college, I ran headlong into our country's great cultural divide. Raised in rural America, and having acquired perspectives and practices related to a strong Protestant faith, I found that many professors had little use for some of them. Wanting to do well in school, I gave the professors the secular perspectives they wanted and kept the faith-based ones to myself.

After completing my undergraduate education in 1980, I traveled behind the Iron Curtain once again. I went to Poland to teach English composition to scientists. I chose Poland because of the great ferment in the country and its many cultural contrasts to the United States. Most adults had full-time jobs and also had to queue up to purchase their food and household supplies for fifteen to twenty hours a week. They lived in small apartments and remained poor no matter what they did. Their government prohibited travel to Western countries and censored their communications, news, books, and periodicals.

Just before my arrival, Karol Wojtyła, the charismatic cardinal from Cracow, became Pope John Paul II. His election gave the Poles tremendous confidence. While I was there, most Poles went on strike and gathered in the churches to protest their living standards and lack of freedom. All my students were members of Solidarity, the first independent labor union in a Soviet-bloc country. President Reagan and Margaret Thatcher encouraged and supported the Poles strikes and protests. Lech Wałęsa, Pope John Paul II, and Cardinal Wyszyński, the Roman Catholic Primate of Poland, orchestrated it.

Cosmos and *The Dragons of Eden* by Carl Sagan were two of the several books that I had brought with me. They described the evolution of the universe and human intelligence. I read and reflected upon these books and all I had learned in the prior three years. The better acquainted I became with science's explanation of the universe and life, the more I realized my childhood faith rested on incredulous, unsubstantiated stories of the past. My faith conveniently dismissed important scientific perspectives that better explained the origin and workings of the universe and life.

Awestruck with the cosmos and science and skeptical of many religious tenets, I begrudgingly underwent the religious-to-secular transformation that millions of other people have undergone. Gradually, I came to favor scientific thought over the faith-based tenets.

By age twenty-six, I had traveled to forty-five states and twenty-six countries. I had lived in two states and two countries and completed my BS and MS degrees, and the courses for a PhD. Plus, I read some two hundred of the world's most thought-provoking books. I had detected the primary question that has preoccupied me for years, confronted our cultural divide, and embraced evidence-based knowledge.

Through my exposure to various cultures and thought, I encountered many conflicting perspectives and practices. As someone who is inquisitive, contemplative, and who values intellectual consistency, the conflicts did not sit well with me. They forced me to evaluate many of my childhood paradigms and grapple with many questions. For example, what is universal to human life and what is particular to a group, locale, or country? How did the universe and life arise? What are the implications of the perspectives and narratives of science? Why do some people flourish while others subsist? Why do some people make so many decisions that inflict future suffering upon themselves and others?

What fueled the extraordinary rise of the English Commonwealth countries, the United States, Western Europe, Japan, South Korea, Taiwan, Hong Kong, and Singapore? Why did our country's founders so distrust concentrations of power? Authoritarianism or democracy, nationalism or federalism, capitalism, socialism, or communism—what works best? What enables large middle classes to emerge and flourish?

Why are conservatives and liberals sometimes right and sometimes wrong? Why are the results of so many public policies antithetical to their supporters' intentions? What fuels growth? How do we prevent recessions, depressions, and inflation?

Despite my shattered paradigms and many questions, I functioned reasonably well, drawing upon the values and habits of my youth. However, when my wife placed our son in my arms, I experienced a bit of a crisis. He came with no instruction book. What was I going to teach him? Given the perspectives and knowledge gained over the last five hundred years, what does a child need to learn? What fosters our health, effectiveness, longevity, civility, and happiness? How do we adapt our lifestyles to live responsibly and do no harm?

These questions and our great cultural divide have haunted me for years. The divide itself separates families, communities, and the citizens of our country. It diminishes our fitness, effectiveness, social cohesiveness, and our children's future. Having spent time on both sides of it, I have friends who have a faith and ones who have no faith. God and traditional Judeo-Christian truths are alive, revered, and the answer to life's problems for those who have faith, whereas God has died and traditional Judeo-Christian perspectives and practices have little validity for those who have no faith.

The great irony of the cultural divide is that each side has something the other lacks. People of faith maintain an empowering culture, and people of science build an empowering knowledge base. People of faith understand that doing the right things yields positive effects, and the people of science understand that life is what we make of it.

For many years, I raised my family, built three businesses, and sat on numerous community, state, and national boards. I read hundreds more books, traveled to many more states and countries, attended educational programs, ran for Congress, and pondered these questions and the divide.

Eventually, I found answers to these questions and a bridge to the cultural divide. I discovered that unless we study the physical and biological sciences in college, we do not generally acquire an evidence-based understanding of the evolution of the universe and life. Most of us lack the interest and maturity to comprehend its implications when we are in high school. If we take the time to understand the narrative, mechanisms, and supporting evidence and integrate the perspectives into our thinking, we can improve our effectiveness and lives immeasurably.

While undergoing this process, I distilled eight Winning Perspectives of the universe and life, or in other words, eight critical views of the cards that nature deals us.

> **Winning Perspectives** are accurate perceptions of reality and conditions of existence. Substantial evidence exists for them. They further our effectiveness and help us identify Winning Practices.

Additionally, I spent years identifying some two hundred Winning Practices.

> **Winning Practices** are actions that positively affect individuals, groups, and/or the environment in the short and long term.

The more populations employ Winning Practices, the more they flourish. The more they use losing practices—the antitheses of Winning Practices—the more they mire themselves in conflict and subsistence.

I have assembled this collection of Winning Perspectives and Practices in a series of four books that may be read individually or sequentially, and a fifth book that contains all of them. The five books of the *Flourish* series are:

- *Toward Truth, Freedom, Fitness, and Decency*

- *Winning Practices of Government and Enterprise*

- *Winning Practices of Families and Education*

- *Winning Practices of Individuals and Groups*

- *Winning Practices of a Free, Fit, and Prosperous People*

This book compares life in Singapore, Switzerland, and the United States and summarizes some of the practices that underlie our country's poor performance. It then discusses eight perspectives that are critical to the identification of Winning Practices.

The second book discusses some problems with democracies and the Winning Practices of Government and Enterprise. The third book describes the Winning Practices of Families and Education, and the fourth book delineates the Winning Practices of Individuals and Groups. The fifth book summarizes all the material of the first four books, and it proposes a new democratic institution to defend, preserve, and evolve our culture.

America is at a critical juncture. As scientists more credibly explain our context, origin, and nature, they discredit religion and cause many people to inadvertently discard faith-based Winning Practices. More-over, as we welcome ever more immigrants into our country and do not convey to them Winning Practices, we erode the prevalence of these practices within our population.

The path forward is relatively clear, but ignorance, errant ideology, and vested interests hinder our progress. Our past success, accumulated wealth, and tremendous capacity to borrow enable us to be foolish for a long time.

Throughout my life, I have negotiated the middle, learning from and perplexing those of the left and the right. If I have done my job nego-tiating this terrain well, conservatives will find many of my thoughts liberal, liberals will find many of them conservative, and moderates will find most of them refreshing.

The *Flourish* series is a synthesis of many of the world's most empowering perspectives and practices. Health, prosperity, long life, and greatly diminished heartache await those who understand, employ, perpetuate, and improve upon these perspectives and practices.

CHAPTER 1

Losing Our Way

We thought we were different . . . more able, prosperous, and blessed. And we were more of those things, as we were more honest, hardworking, and responsible; as we took marriage, parenting, and education more seriously; and as we were more community and country minded.

One of the most telling indications that our country is losing its way is the relative change in American and Chinese living standards between 1990 and 2014. In 1990, American living standards were seventy-five times greater than Chinese living standards. In 2014, they were seven times higher.[1]

Chinese living standards have improved steadily while our living standards have stagnated. Figure 1 shows actual and growing hypothetical U.S. household incomes between 1990–2014. Adjusted for inflation, our real median income has been flat for a generation. If it had increased 3 percent a year during this period, more of a historical norm, it would be $107,000 rather than $54,000!

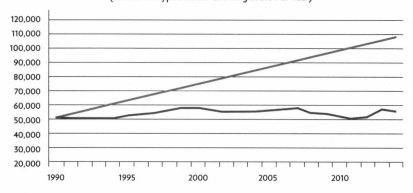

Figure 1: Median Household Income 1990-2015
(Actual vs Hypothetical Growing at 3% Per Year)

United States Census Bureau, Data, Income Data Tables

Table H-8 Median Household Income by State,

https://www.census.gov/data/tables/time-series/demo/income-poverty/historical-income-households.html

Amazingly, the Chinese economy became almost as large as the U.S. economy in 2016. If the two economies continue to grow at their current relative rates, then the Chinese economy will be two times larger than ours in twelve years and four times larger in twenty-four years.

Rising living standards in China are a great thing, but the combination of Chinese ascendency and American decline is not good for Western values and populations. The Chinese have their own interests and values, many of which compete with ours. As China rises and America declines, China will reshape the international order to reflect their interests and values. China will encourage one-party rule around the world rather than constitutional republics and the rule of law. It will encourage state prerogatives over individual rights. It will seize control of South Pacific shipping lanes and make the terms of trade less favorable to other countries. China's currency, the renminbi, may even replace the dollar as the reserve currency of the world, decreasing American living standards an additional 10 to 20 percent.

Rising Chinese living standards and stagnant American living standards are not our only challenges. Radical Islam and the Islamic population growth are also serious problems. While our leaders hesitate to acknowledge it, the Western and Islamic cultures collide. Where we value democratic and secular government, individual rights, and male and female parity, most Islamic leaders value authoritarian and religious rule, religious orthodoxy, and male dominance.

While we may find it incomprehensible that large numbers of Muslims hate us, the fact is that many do. Our promiscuous lifestyles, dysfunctional families, alcohol and drug abuse, and high crime rates are unappealing to them. Our freedoms, gender equality, and religious tolerance undermine their patterns of life. Our priorities, might, and actions thwart their leaders' aspirations.

To these three serious challenges, I would add seven more: (1) a failure to develop and educate many children, (2) a failure to integrate many African Americans, Hispanics, and Muslims in our country, (3) our government's dysfunction and propensity to live beyond its means,

(4) our emissions of large quantities of greenhouse gases, (5) the degradation of ecosystems and groundwater, (6) the eradication of many species, and (7) the tendency for Winning Perspectives and Practices to decrease in prevalence within our culture and losing ones to increase.

While each of these challenges is discussed in more detail later in this and subsequent books, this chapter focuses on our declining vitality and the causes of the decreasing prevalence of Winning Perspectives and Practices within our country.

Inclusion Failures

Our ancestors provided us with a stunning start. Their pragmatism, ideals, and newly minted government were extraordinary. Their courage, hard work, sacrifice, and perseverance were monumental. The only problems with the stunning start were that our ancestors took our country from the Native Americans and some of them enslaved Africans. The institution of slavery and eradication of most Native Americans were travesties. Yes, we have acknowledged the horrific treatment of Native Americans and ended slavery, but we have yet to integrate many Native and African Americans into our communities.

Our destruction of the Native American culture was both an unfortunate genocide and a great lost opportunity. Had we treated Native Americans more honorably and shared more of this vast continent with them, we might have acquired their great reverence and respect for the environment. We might have harmed our environment less, emitted less carbon and fewer pollutants, be healthier, and have a brighter future.

Our inclusion failures were not only at the start, though. They have occurred in every decade since, and they remain with us. Segregation, discrimination, and education dysfunction have created reservoirs of mistrust and animosity, and islands of depravity. They have created destructive subcultures, unsafe neighborhoods, broken families, widespread alcohol and drug addiction, and millions of poorly parented children.

The world over, majorities naturally discriminate against minorities. People unconsciously and consciously favor those most like them.

This behavior is instinctual. "Birds of a feather flock together" and "you can tell a zebra by its stripes" are adages indicative of this tendency. And while this instinct may have served hunter-gatherers well, it no longer serves us well. A people comprised of different races, ethnicities, and creeds must overcome discriminatory behavior with education, training, and effective recourse.

The lack of a clean start and our integration failures divide us. They diminish minority actualization and contribution. They increase our social welfare burdens and decrease our living standards. They reduce the prevalence of Winning Practices within our culture. They diminish our social cohesion and our ability to overcome challenges.

The Change in the Election of U.S. Senators

> The powers delegated by the proposed Constitution to the federal government are few and defined. Those which are to remain in the State governments are numerous and indefinite.[2]
>
> —James Madison

James Madison was a primary author of the Constitution and Federalist Papers, as well as the fourth president of the United States. He and our other founders limited the scope and power of the federal government in the Constitution. This changed, though, when the U.S. Congress and the states passed the Seventeenth Amendment in 1913. Before the amendment, state legislatures chose the U.S. Senators. After it, the people of each state elected them. Where state legislators wanted to preserve state power and limit federal power, most citizens lack these self-interests.

Except for a ten-year period around the Civil War, our federal government's expenditures as a percent of GNP were less than 4 percent for the first 125 years of our nation's history. As Figure 2 illustrates, the passage of the Seventeenth Amendment changed this. Over the subsequent hundred years, federal expenditures as a percent of GNP grew more than nine-fold—from 2.5 percent to 21 percent.

The monopolistic federal government was relatively small before the seventeenth amendment in 1913. It had a few specified powers, and the numerous competing state governments had broad powers. Since 1913, our federal government has expanded its powers significantly and has become a wasteful, inefficient, and corrupt colossus. It now has broad unchecked powers. It regulates every aspect of our life, burdening us and stifling our economy.

Figure 2: U.S. Federal Spending
(As a Percent of GNP from 1800-2015)

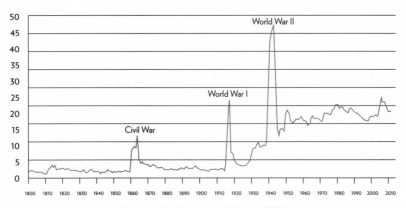

Measuring Worth, Data Sets, US Nominal GDP
https://www.measuringworth.com/
Government Spending, Download Spending Data
Multiyear Download of US Government Spending 1800–2015
http://www.usgovernmentspending.com/download_multi_year_1792_2015USb_17s2li001mcn_F0f

Since 1913, the story of the state governments is more mixed. States like New York, Illinois, and California have created larger governments, stifling the improvement of many residents' living standards. On the other hand, states like Florida, Indiana, South Carolina, and Texas have maintained smaller governments, enabling their residents' living standards to improve steadily.

Ending the state legislature check on the federal government was one of our greatest mistakes, as unchecked government weighs a people down just as too much overhead and debt weigh a company down. You only need to compare the great gains that people made and continue to make throughout the world when their government spending as a percent of GNP is in the 5–15 percent range to the small increases that occur when this ratio exceeds 20 percent. The histories of Canada, U.S., Western Europe, and Japan all demonstrate this reality.

Presidential Constitutional Failings

Whether we like presidents Theodore Roosevelt, Wilson, Franklin Roosevelt, Truman, Johnson, Nixon, Bush 41, Clinton, Bush 43, and Obama and their policies, their flagrant failures to defend the Constitution and abuses of power should trouble us.

World history is one long chronology of government abuse of its citizens. Only with the signing of the Magna Carta by King John in 1215, the signing of the Petition of Right by King Charles I in 1628, and the passage of the Bill of Rights in 1689 did English-speaking people have freedom from the arbitrary and oppressive yoke of their rulers. Only with the adoption of the Articles of Federation in 1777, the Constitution of the United States of America in 1787, and the first ten amendments known as the Bill of Rights in 1791 did our ancestors free us of this yoke.

From 1777 to 1900, Americans appreciated their constitution—its separation of power and checks on power and specified institutions, procedures, and requirements. Up until then, most of our government leaders took their oath of office seriously and preserved, protected, and defended the Constitution. Unfortunately, this changed with the election of Theodore Roosevelt and has continued unabated ever since.

This flagrant failure to uphold and defend the document that defines the separations of power, checks on power, governing processes, and our rights jeopardizes our freedoms. Common presidential misuse of the federal government and public treasury to reward political supporters and punish political opponents polarizes us. Any expediency and gains from these activities are more than offset by the long-term adverse effects of these actions. Brion McClanahan catalogues and explains many presidential failings and abuses of power in his book *9 Presidents Who Screwed Up America*. Some of these presidential failings and abuses of power appear in Figure 3 on page 20.

The Constitution of the United States is one of the most important documents ever written. Hundreds of millions of Americans and other people around the world have had much better lives because of it. If you have not read it, I highly recommend that you do so. It is ingenious, straightforward, and understandable—and only about twenty-five pages long.

Basically, "the people" give the federal government its legitimacy. They grant to it a few specified powers and vest all other governing powers to the state governments. Here is the list of the few powers that the people give the federal government:

- *Levy uniformly applied taxes and duties,*

- *Borrow money,*

- *Coin money, regulate its value, and punish counterfeiting,*

- *Define and punish unlawful offenses,*

- *Establish judiciaries inferior to the Supreme Court,*

- *Create standards of weights and measures,*

- *Regulate commerce,*

- *Establish uniform bankruptcy laws,*

- *Create uniform rules of naturalization,*

- *Secure author and inventor copy and patent rights for limited times,*

- *Make laws regarding acquired lands,*

- *Create the set of laws necessary to carry out the powers specified by the Constitution,*

- *Build roads,*

- *Establish post offices,*

- *Call forth a militia to execute the laws of the land, suppress insurrections, and repel invasions,*

- *Support an army and navy, and*

- *Declare war and make treaties.*

The framers of our government knew the Constitution and its specified institutions, procedures, and requirements were imperfect. They knew the country's needs would change over time. Thus, they included a provision where two-thirds of Congress or two-thirds of the states could request an amendment to the Constitution, and three-quarters of the state legislatures could ratify or defeat a proposed amendment. Our founders created a procedure that gives us time to thoroughly consider a change and that requires widespread support. They set the hurdles high for changing the Constitution, perhaps too high, as the hurdle has only been met twenty-seven times in 220 years.

What are some of the ways that twentieth- and twenty-first-century presidents have failed to preserve, protect, and defend the Constitution? Starting with Theodore Roosevelt and contrary to the separation of the legislative, executive, and judicial functions in the Constitution, numerous presidents have used the executive office, presidential favors, and executive orders to push legislative agendas. Teddy Roosevelt's Square Deal, seizure of 230 million acres of land, and 1,081 executive orders; Woodrow Wilson's New Freedom legislation and 1,803 executive orders; and Franklin Roosevelt's New Deal and 3,522 executive orders, one of which confiscated much of the gold in the country, are all examples of presidential violations of the Constitution. Lyndon Johnson's Great Society legislation and 325 executive orders and George W. Bush's 291 executive orders, many of which violated fundamental American rights, are other serious examples of presidential violations of the Constitution.

Several presidents have supported the federal government's assumption of powers that "the people" never granted to it. Franklin Roosevelt used the influence of the presidency to enact Food Stamps, Welfare, and Social Security; Lyndon Johnson to involve the federal involvement in education, healthcare, the arts, and public broadcasting; and Barack Obama to control the free market healthcare system.

Some presidents have created executive agencies with the ability to create regulations, execute them, and adjudicate them. Woodrow Wilson did this with the Federal Trade Commission. Richard Nixon did this with the Occupational Safety and Health Administration and Environmental Protection Agency.

Some presidents treated some groups more favorably or unfavorably than other groups. Woodrow Wilson exempted agriculture and labor unions from antitrust laws with the Clayton Trust Act of 1914, and Barack Obama used the Internal Revenue Agency against conservative groups.

Several recent presidents also violated their oaths to preserve, protect, and defend the Constitution with their selective enforcement of federal laws. Barack Obama, one of the most unlawful presidents in our country's history, made appointments to oversee the executive departments, National Labor Relations Board, and federal courts without congressional consent. He unlawfully delayed the implementation of the Affordable Care Act twenty-eight times. He did not enforce many drug laws and released thousands of federal prisoners. And worst of all, he not only failed to enforce the immigration and naturalization laws, but he also encouraged foreigners to violate them by (a) restricting the 287(g) program that permits police officers to apprehend illegal immigrants who are stopped for other crimes, (b) ignoring the thirty-one sanctuary cities that protect illegal immigrants, and (c) curtailing funding for a program designed to find visitors who overstay their visas.[3]

The Constitution of the United States of America gives Congress the power to declare war and the president the power to make treaties. Theodore Roosevelt used the military in the Panama revolution without a declaration of war from Congress. Woodrow Wilson used the military in several Latin American countries and Russia. Lyndon Johnson did this in Vietnam, Ronald Reagan in Grenada, and Barack Obama in Libya and Syria. Harry Truman used the U.S. military as an agent of the United Nations, and Bill Clinton used it forty-one times around the world. Historian Brion McClanahan writes:

> The slew of executive legislative initiatives since the 1930s has forced Americans to believe that American government is executive government, regardless of political party. We feel confident in our guy in office and think little of the potential ramifications should our guy be out of office and the other guy takes his place. Republicans who insist on impeaching Obama for his unconstitutional acts are the same who defended George W. Bush and his unconstitutional acts, and vice versa. Inconsistency and excessive partisanship—something George Washington warned against in his Farewell Address—has inflicted terrible damage on the American experiment in republican self-government.[4]

This is not to pass judgment on the intentions of these presidents or suggest that we do not need to deal with crises quickly, end discrimination, look out for the poor, help some seniors with retirement expenses, preserve habitats, curb pollution, and defend ourselves. It is only to suggest that there are approaches consistent with the Constitution to do all these things, ways that I describe in the next book in the series, *Flourish: Winning Practices of Government and Enterprise.*

It is to suggest that we should celebrate the presidents who fulfilled the responsibilities of the presidency and conscientiously preserved, protected, and defended our system of government, and be more critical of the ones who used the office and crises of their times to advance their political agendas. Thomas Jefferson, John Tyler, Grover Cleveland, and Calvin Coolidge are excellent examples of defenders of the Constitution who we should venerate more, and Theodore Roosevelt, Woodrow

Wilson, Franklin Roosevelt, Lyndon Johnson, George W. Bush, and Barack Obama are examples of presidents who we should venerate less.

People wonder why our federal government is so expensive, intrusive in our lives, partisan, and dysfunctional. While there are many reasons, certainly our failure to hold our presidents accountable to the Constitution is a primary one. For over half of the presidents in the twentieth and twenty-first centuries to take the oath to uphold the Constitution and then to repeatedly violate it does not bode well for our country. For Congress not to impeach these presidents is irresponsible. For the press not to expose these presidents' constitutional violations is unconscionable. These failures set horrible precedents for future presidents, elected representatives, and journalists.

Figure 3: Presidential Constitutional Failings

THEODORE ROOSEVELT

The Square Deal Legislative Initiative

The Food and Drug and the Meat Inspection Acts of 1906

Proclamations to Seize 230 Million Acres of Land

The Use of the Military in the Panama Revolution

WOODROW WILSON

The New Freedom Agenda Approach toward the Constitution

The Federal Reserve Act of 1913

Clayton Trust Act of 1914

Federal Trade Commission Act of 1914

The Federal Loan Administration of 1916

Selective Service Act of 1917

War Industries Board, War Labor Board, Federal Fuel Administration

The Sedition Act of 1918

The Nationalization of Radio and Committee of Public Information

Use of the Military in Several Counties

FRANKLIN ROOSEVELT

Agricultural Adjustment and National Industrial Recovery Acts of 1933

Civilian Works Administration and Civilian Conservation Corps

Executive Order Confiscating Gold in 1933

The National Housing Act of 1934

Labor Relations and Export Boards

Banking Act of 1935

Social Security Act of 1935

The Supreme Court Packing Plan and Threat in 1937

The National War Labor Board and the War Manpower Commission

The Offices of Economic Stabilization and War Information in 1942

HARRY TRUMAN

The Seizure of Numerous Private Businesses

The Continuation of Price Controls after the War

The Appropriation of Large Sums for the Marshall Plan and Cold War

The Use of the United States Military as Agent of the United Nations

LYNDON JOHNSON

Clean Air and Endangered Species Preservation Acts of 1963 and 1966

Economic Opportunities and Food Stamp Acts of 1964

The Elementary and Secondary Education Act of 1965

Higher Education and Appalachian Region Development Acts of 1965

The Social Security Act of 1965, adding Medicare and Medicaid

Housing and Urban Development Act of 1965

Water Quality Act and Solid Waste Disposal Acts of 1965

The National Foundation of the Arts and Humanities Act of 1965

The Public Broadcasting Act of 1967

The Bilingual Education Act of 1968

The Escalation of the War in Vietnam without a Declaration of War

RICHARD NIXON

National Environmental Policy Act of 1969

Clean Air Act of 1970

Department of Interior Creation of 642 National Parks

Occupational Safety and Health Act of 1970

Enforcement of School Busing

Established Racial Goals and Time Tables that Were in Essence Quotas

Education Amendments of 1972 and Title IX

Ended Bretton Woods, Igniting Inflation and Spawning Economic Bubbles

Myth of Executive Privilege and the Watergate Cover-up

GEORGE W. BUSH

USA Patriot Act of 2001

Invasion of Iraq without a Congressional Declaration of War

No Child Left Behind Act of 2001

Medicare Act of 2003

Troubled Asset Relief Program of 2008

Housing and Economic Recovery Act of 2008

Executive Orders Violating Basic American Rights

BARACK OBAMA

Appointments to Oversee Agencies without Congressional Consent

Granted Work Waivers to Welfare Recipients

Stripped the Creditors of GM and Chrysler of Their Money

Moratorium on Offshore Drilling

Patient Protection and Affordable Care Act of 2010

Delayed Implementation of the ACA Unlawfully 28 Times

Used the IRS Against Conservative Groups

Unlawful Appointments to the National Labor Relations Board

Illegal Appointments to the Consumer Protection Board

Circumvented the Freedom of Information Act

Ordered a Company Plant Closed and Nonunion Workers Fired

Refused to Prosecute Violators of Drug Laws

Encouraged Violations of the Immigration and Naturalization Laws

Use of the Military in Libya and Syria without Declarations of War

When government leaders violate our Constitution and our laws, we must impeach them. When they ignore the unconstitutional and unlawful actions of our presidents, we must not reelect them. When journalists ignore these unconstitutional and unlawful actions, we must boycott their organizations. If we impeached a couple of presidents, did not reelect a few more representatives, and reduced our patronage of these news organizations, these irresponsible behaviors would end. Failure to do these things places everything we hold dear in jeopardy. As James Madison wrote:

> I believe there are more instances of the abridgment of the
> freedom of the people by gradual and silent encroachments
> of those in power than by violent and sudden usurpations.[5]

We have always prided ourselves on being "a nation ruled by laws, not people." Certainly, this is less the case now than in the past, and this should trouble us. For as the integrity of our government goes, so the integrity of our people goes. And as the integrity of both go, so our freedoms, our economy, and wellbeing go.

Supreme Court Constitutional Failings

Constitutional decoupling involves the periodic failure of the U.S. Supreme Court to strike down unconstitutional legislation and executive actions. It results from presidential appointments of justices who are more interested in advancing political agendas than upholding the Constitution. It enables Congress to usurp many state powers and the Executive Branch to usurp judicial and legislative powers.

James Madison was very clear on the limited, specified powers of the federal government and the intended interpretation of the "general welfare" clause:

> With respect to the words "general welfare," I have
> always regarded them as qualified by the detail of powers

connected with them. To take them in a literal and unlimited sense would be a metamorphosis of the Constitution
into a character which there is a host of proofs was not
contemplated by its creators.[6]

Who would have foreseen that a group of progressives would
transform our federal government with a reinterpretation of these two
words? It took over a century, a national crisis, an activist president,
and a cohort of liberal judges, but this did finally happen during the
Franklin Delano Roosevelt presidency. And like water breaching a dike,
once the general welfare clause was reinterpreted, the powers of the federal government grew unceasingly. They expanded so much that since
the 1960s the Legislative Branch routinely creates unconstitutional
laws, the Executive Branch routinely acts in unconstitutional ways,
and the Supreme Court routinely fails to nullify these laws and acts.

These Supreme Court failures now permit Congress to legislate,
tax, and spend in ways that favor some groups over others. They allow
the federal and state governments to interfere with private contracts and
redistribute wealth. They permit Congress to pass poorly defined laws
and let regulatory agencies fill in the details. They allow the Executive
Branch to interpret laws and judge violations of the laws, and the federal
and state governments to seize private property for economic gain. They
give government and institutions the right to use racial preferences.
Detail regarding some of the Supreme Court constitutional failings can
be found in Appendix B.

Some would argue that these changes were needed. My response
is, if this were the case, then the Supreme Court should have upheld
the Constitution, and the legislature should have made the changes
via well-conceived amendments to the Constitution. As the Constitution stipulates, only the states and representatives of the people should
expand the power of the federal government. Individual presidents and
five justices should not do this on their own.

Special Interest Government

With the state legislature check on the growth of the federal government destroyed in 1913 and numerous other constitutional checks destroyed by the Supreme Court in the 1930s, the federal government's expenditures have grown from less than 5 percent to 21 percent of GNP in the last hundred years. Now special interests buy elected officials, and elected officials buy their constituents' votes. Elected officials borrow, tax, and spend recklessly, and they create the conditions to stagnate rather than to flourish.

As federal legislation and expenditures grow, special interests, protective of them, grow. To see this, think of the importance of the federal government to Social Security, Medicaid, Welfare, and Food Stamp recipients, as well as public sector contractors, unions, and employees. When the federal government is small and/or does not deliver preferential status and so many services, those advocating for them are few or do not exist. However, as soon as the federal government becomes large, influential, and preferential, powerful special interests form to protect and expand federal expenditures and preferential treatment.

Crony capitalism is a form of special interest government where business leaders and government officials help one another in ways that hurt taxpayers and consumers. Crony capitalism occurs when business leaders make large campaign contributions to candidates who do favors for them. The favors may take the form of supporting oligopolistic market concentrations, supporting legislation that is advantageous to the businesses of the contributors, or awarding government contracts and grants to these businesses. While some of these favors are advantageous to everyone, most of them benefit one or more businesses and increase the cost of products and services to taxpayers and consumers.

Unionization also creates special interest government. Like crony capitalism, unionization enables union leaders and some government officials to help one another in ways that hurt taxpayers, enterprises, and consumers. It enables union leaders to make large campaign contributions to candidates and incentivize the candidates to do favors for them. The favors take the form of legislation that increases the ability of unions to extract additional money and benefits from employers and taxpayers. While this seems fine to many, the problem is that the favors decrease the competitiveness of enterprises and increase the cost of public and private products and services.

When people allow their central government to become large, it ceases to be a government of the people and becomes a government of special interests. It ceases to respond to citizens' needs and instead responds to special interests.

Less Faith-Community Relevance

As science has exposed more of the cause-and-effect relationships of the universe, life, and related processes, it inadvertently has decreased the credibility of religious teachings. It has caused religious teachings and their systems of rewards and penalties—like a day of judgment and an eternal life in heaven or hell—to lose sway first over liberals, then moderates, and more recently many conservatives. When religious institutions lose progressive members, they lose ability to evolve. They lose ability to keep their perspectives, practices, heroes, and art forms relevant to new generations. They lose ability to help people do the right thing and act in an honest, responsible, civil, and considerate manner.

We see the declining influence of faith communities in the change in Christian church attendance the last fifty years. Where over 60 percent of the U.S. population regularly attended services in 1960, less than 20 percent of the population regularly attended services in 2005.[7] The reduced influence of a primary institution on over 40 percent of the U.S. population parallels the decrease of honesty and civility in our culture.

Less Integrity, Responsibility, and Civility

As faith communities lose relevance, many people's integrity, responsibility, and civility decline. If other institutions do not teach and positively reinforce these behaviors, they become less prevalent within our population. Gradually and imperceptibly, we become less truthful, responsible, civil, and productive, and we become more self-centered and short-term oriented.

In the last fifty years, spouses have become less committed to each other. Parents have become less respectful of principals, teachers, and coaches. Children have become less respectful of parents, teachers, and police. Employers and employees have become less conscientious about their responsibilities, and people in general have become less concerned about doing what is best for others.

How irresponsible, uncivil, and corrupt are we? Twenty-five percent of Americans age eighteen and older regularly engage in heavy drinking.[8] Thirty-eight percent of Americans ages eighteen to twenty-five smoke, and thirty-six percent use illicit drugs.[9] Fifteen percent of Americans gamble at least once a week.[10]

The American Sexual Health Association estimates sexually transmitted diseases are prevalent in 110 million Americans, twenty million new infections occur each year, and more than half of all Americans will contract a sexually transmitted disease sometime in their life.[11]

Some 66 percent of all traffic fatalities are caused by road rage and aggressive driving.[12] The U.S. ranks seventy-fifth among 120 countries in incidence of crime. Nicaragua, Saudi Arabia, Israel, Azerbaijan, Turkey, Ethiopia, India, and Russia all indicate lower incidence of crime than the U.S.[13] On the World Corruption Perception Index, the U.S. ranks seventeenth among nations.[14]

The relatively widespread acceptance and use of offensive language, alcohol, illegal drugs, promiscuity, and gambling among high school students, college students, and the general population is not indicative of a people concerned about their children's development or a people on the rise. Such incidences of losing practices are indicative of subsistence and decline, and they are much less prevalent in Switzerland, Singapore, and many other developed countries.

Promiscuity and the Decline of Marriage

If we examine our country's history through the 1950s, we find that most men and women married at a relatively young age, the marriages remained intact for life, and most children had the benefit of two parents. We now find that marriage rates have fallen by two-thirds, and separation and divorce rates have increased three times since the 1950s.[15] With the declining influence of religion, the development of highly reliable forms of birth control, the changing roles of women, and the implementation of generous welfare programs, the incidents of promiscuity, cohabitation, and divorce have increased precipitously. Now, half of our marriages fail and more than half of our children grow up in a single-parent household and nontraditional family.

These new patterns of life do not negatively impact us all equally. They impact college graduates less than non–college graduates. Harvard professor of public policy Robert Putnam writes:

> In the college-educated, upper third of American society, a "neo-traditional" marriage pattern has emerged. It mirrors the 1950s family in many respects, except that both partners now typically work outside of the home, they delay marriage and childbearing until their careers are under way, and they divide domestic duties more evenly. . . . In the high-school-educated, lower third of the population, by contrast, a new, more kaleidoscopic pattern began to emerge in which childbearing became increasingly disconnected from marriage, and sexual partnerships became less durable.[16]

While the new relational mores affect college-educated couples and their children less, their adverse impact on the economically-challenged lower third of our population should concern all of us, as no people can thrive when a set of mores results in one-third of the children growing up in dysfunctional families, neighborhoods, and schools.

Poorly Parented Children

While some parents who maintain healthy, lifelong marriages do a poor job parenting children and some parents who separate and typically have multiple mates do a good job parenting, the reality is that the more traditional families generally do a much better job parenting. Parents of these families usually have greater commitments to each other and their children than those of nontraditional ones. They provide children more parental time, resources, and stability; a healthier balance of nurture, discipline, and expectation; and greater educational and mentoring opportunities.

Professor Putnam indicates that 6 percent of children in the U.S. lived in nontraditional families during the 1960s, but over half of all children will live in one now. He also indicates that children with parents in the lowest educational quartile are roughly two times more likely to live with one parent during their childhood than those with parents in the highest quartile.[17] And again, while some nontraditional families do a fantastic job raising their children, the research indicates that most do not do so well. Children of nontraditional families usually are shortchanged. Professor Putnam writes:

> Children who grow up without their biological father perform worse on standardized tests, earn lower grades, and stay in school for fewer years, regardless of race and class. They are also more likely to demonstrate behavioral problems such as shyness, aggression, and psychological problems such as increased anxiety and depression. Children who spend part of their childhood in a single-mother home are also more likely to have sex earlier and to become young, single parents, re-creating the cycle.
>
> Children in divorced or remarried families face distinctive challenges, partly because their families' limited resources must be spread across more than one household, and partly because their parents' lingering grievances, and

physical and emotional distance from one another, hamper effective communication and coordination. Multi-partner fertility is associated with less parental involvement, less extended kin involvement, and more friction, jealousy, and competition, especially when there are children from different partnerships living in the same household.[18]

Marriage, intact families, and good parenting matter a great deal! So much of our individual and collective fitness depend on them that I devote over half of the third book in the *Flourish* series to the critical Winning Practices related to them.

Unionization of Education

In the 1960s, the Democratic Party and union leaders saw an opportunity to unionize the people who worked in the public sector. Undoubtedly, public employee compensation was sometimes low and some school boards and superintendents were undesirable employers. Yet, some fifty years later, it is painfully clear that the ill effects of this change far outweigh the benefits.

Primary and secondary education have become less effective and costlier in many parts of the country. Proportionally fewer children can do math and read, write, and speak well. Proportionally fewer children have Winning Perspectives, possess empowering habits, and utilize Winning Practices. Proportionally fewer children graduate from high school, are well equipped to parent children, have productive careers, and become responsible citizens. Collectively, we spend much more on education for children and obtain poorer results.

Union work rules, seniority-based compensation, and tenure hinder the employment of the ablest administrators and teachers. They prevent administrators from adjusting teachers' compensation in accordance with their performance. They make it extremely difficult for administrators to terminate poor-performing teachers, and they elevate compensation packages above those of comparable private sector employees.

Schools matter! They need to perform at a high level. We are under their tutelage for thirteen years. Parents and schools nurture and develop us. They prepare us for success or failure. They make us individually and collectively fit or weak.

Liberalization of Education

Union work rules, seniority-based compensation, and tenure change administrators' and teachers' interests. They politicize education and cause administrators and teachers to support the candidates for public office who readily support unions. Thus, the number of administrators and teachers who register as Democrats and donate to the Democratic Party increases, and the number who register as Republicans and give to the Republican Party decreases.

After a couple of generations of this, public education is filled with administrators and teachers who look unfavorably on many of the Winning Practices that enable us to thrive. More and more public educators dislike the limited, decentralized federal government upon which our freedoms and living standards depend. They dislike the competition and meritocracy upon which free enterprise and free markets depend. They discard proven educational approaches that have yielded good results and adopt unproven ones that yield poor results. Many are hesitant to discipline children and uphold basic behavioral and academic standards.

Liberalized public schools do not group students by their ability or help children form as many empowering habits as in the past. They mainstream disruptive students. They often do not give children credit for doing homework, and some forbid teachers from even giving homework. Many give children who perform poorly on tests multiple opportunities to retake them.

Liberalized public schools dumb down curriculum, inflate grades, and advance many students who fail to master the material. They promote cultural relativism, nonjudgmentalism, and multiculturalism, concepts that I discuss later in this chapter. They do not give children a sense of the things that enable us to prosper, like shared values; a constitutional, limited, representative federal government; free enterprise; and free markets.

Not having a healthy mix of conservatives, moderates, and progressives administrating our public schools and teaching our children contributes to much of the dysfunction of our schools and country.

Social Justice Missteps

Given the genocide, slavery, discrimination, segregation, and limitations on women in our history, many of our greatest heroes are people who devoted their lives to the pursuit of social justice. People like Horace Mann, Frederick Douglass, Harriet Beecher Stowe, Booker T. Washington, Elizabeth Cady Stanton, Susan B. Anthony, John Steinbeck, Jackie Robinson, Martin Luther King, and Betty Friedan worked tirelessly to break discriminatory barriers and improve the lives of minorities, women, and poor people. These heroes were either victims of injustice or unusually sensitive to injustice. And to the best of my knowledge, they all employed honorable means to curtail the injustices of their time.

The pursuit of social justice is advantageous and laudable when it (a) makes us more conscious of injustice, (b) breaks senseless barriers and advances opportunity, and (c) improves our attitudes, norms, and laws. It is advantageous and laudable when it empowers individuals, increases personal responsibility, advances education and work opportunities, and furthers civility, social cohesion, and prosperity for all.

On the other hand, the pursuit of social justice is disadvantageous when it (a) employs deception, lawlessness, and violence, (b) favors some people over others, (c) undermines and excuses personal responsibility, (d) seeks equal outcomes, and (e) furthers animosity, division, and dependence.

Safe neighborhoods, school choice, free remedial educational opportunities, antidiscrimination laws, and work opportunities are all approaches to social justice that are advantageous to the larger population. Tolerance of crime and discrimination; free housing, food, healthcare, education, and pensions; tolerance and even encouragement of illegal immigration; lower admission standards; excusing disruptive behavior in schools; irresponsible borrowing, taxing, and spending; and irresponsible monetary policy are all approaches to social justice that are disadvantageous to the larger population.

While many politicians have employed social justice concerns to garner political support, our citizens largely steered clear of supporting the counterproductive approaches until the presidencies of Franklin Roosevelt, Harry Truman, Lyndon Johnson, Richard Nixon, and Barack Obama. Our citizens avoided the disadvantageous approaches for over 150 years, but as our regard for the Constitution waned, opportunistic politicians opened Pandora's box, started employing the disadvantageous approaches, and sowed the seeds of discord, polarization, and decline.

Relativism, Nonjudgmentalism, and Multiculturalism

Relativism is the belief that truth exists in relation to culture, society, and historical context. Nonjudgmentalism and multiculturalism are logical extensions of relativism. Nonjudgmentalism is the idea that we should not evaluate or judge others and their behaviors because they are a product of their culture and context. Multiculturalism is the idea that all cultures are equally meritorious. The appeal of relativism, nonjudgmentalism, and multiculturalism is that there is an element of truth to them, they further tolerance, and they make everybody feel good about themselves.

The problems with relativism, nonjudgmentalism, and multiculturalism are first, they are not completely true. Second, what works "best" is not always relative; sometimes it is universal. Third, some cultures or collection of perspectives and practices further people's wellbeing better than other ones, and we must be able to judge the desirability of perspectives and practices.

Relativism, nonjudgmentalism, and multiculturalism discourage the discrimination between winning and losing perspectives and practices, opening people up to a whole array of counterproductive per-spectives and practices. Their absurdity becomes more apparent in the extreme, as in being unable to determine the relative desirability of the Swiss and Haitian cultures, and Singaporean and North Korean cultures. Yale professor and *New York Times* columnist David Brooks writes of this cultural challenge in his column, "The Cost of Relativism":

> We now have multiple generations of people caught in recurring feedback loops of economic stress and family breakdown . . . It's not only money and better policy that are missing in these circles; it's norms . . . These norms weren't destroyed because of people with bad values. They were destroyed by a plague of nonjudgmentalism, which refused to assert that one way of behaving was better than another.[19]

With the liberalization of education, relativism, nonjudgmentalism, and multiculturalism became actively promoted in our public schools and universities. Excessive tolerance and the idea that all cultures are equally desirable supplanted a mature discrimination between winning and losing perspectives and practices as well as the idea that the American culture had something important to offer immigrants. Our public schools and universities also undermined our founders' objective of *e pluribus unum*, or "from many, one," that served us so well for almost two centuries. They supplanted the practice of immigrants "melting" and becoming American, and they made diversity more important than social cohesion.

Rather than pushing relativism, nonjudgmentalism, and multicul-turalism on our children, we would be better served to teach them that diversity, social cohesion, and Winning Practices are all critical to our fitness and wellbeing. We should expose them to many cultures and teach them to identify Winning Perspectives and Practices. Then, we should encourage them to adopt the Winning Perspectives and Practices and to jettison losing ones.

Declining Discipline, Poor Habits, and Less Learning

Greater general affluence, the unionization and liberalization of education, and the adoption of relativism, multiculturalism, and non-judgmentalism have caused parents and schools to be less concerned about children's habits and much more permissive. The days of showing respect for one's elders, controlling emotional outbursts, and immediately responding to the directives of parents, teachers, and other authorities without attitude have passed for many young people. Completing one's assignments on time and doing well on a test the first time are no longer common expectations of parents and teachers. The days of always being at work on time and not missing work have also passed for many adults.

We have now entered an era of little discipline, poor habits, and less learning. We hype our children's self-esteem, encourage them to vocalize their feelings, and let them do whatever they want. In doing this, we deny them the opportunity to learn self-control, to learn to defer gratification, and to form empowering habits. We set them up for a lifetime of failure and disappointment rather than numerous successes and steady forward progress.

Oligopoly and Monopoly

When competition, free enterprise, and free markets prevail, buyers and sellers have choices, reputations matter, and people have incentives to do the right things.

Free enterprise and free markets serve us well until governments allow a few buyers or sellers to dominate a market. When sellers concentrate to the point where three or fewer sellers have most of the customers, buyers lose. Sellers overcharge, are less responsive, and innovate less. Similarly, when buyers concentrate to the point where three or fewer generate most of the orders, sellers lose. Buyers underpay and dictate the terms.

Over the years, we have seen what happens when buyers or sellers concentrate. We have seen this with the railroads, energy providers, auto manufacturers, telephone companies, airlines, healthcare providers, cable companies, and numerous other industries. Each time a few companies dominate a market, consumers lose. They pay higher prices, receive poor quality products and service, and have few alternatives.

Free enterprise and markets work best when there are numerous buyers and sellers in each market. They only fail us when externalities exist and on the rare occasions when human emotion and excesses create extreme overbuying or overselling. In such situations, prudent actions by governments and central banks can mitigate the negative effects of externalities and human emotions, and restore the orderly function of markets. I discuss roles for government and central banks relative to orderly market function later in the book. The important point now is that governments, enterprises, markets, and people become predatory when power concentrates.

Offshoring

Starting in the 1960s, several companies found it advantageous to move their operations to Japan, Hong Kong, Singapore, South Korea, and Taiwan, and later in the 1980s 1990s, and 2000s to China, India, Indonesia, and Vietnam. And rather than looking introspectively for the causes of the exodus, our leaders conveniently indicated that the inexpensive, industrious labor of these countries was the cause. While the low-cost labor of Asia has been a factor, there exist other less commonly discussed causes of offshoring.

First, the U.S. has had, and continues to have, one of the highest corporate tax rates in the world. A 10 to 15 percent higher corporate income tax is a serious competitive disadvantage over time.

Second, the U.S. federal, state, and local governments have some of the most onerous regulations in the world. Collectively, these regulations slow the transaction of business and significantly increase the cost of doing business.

Third, unions in the U.S. have been a problem. Private sector unions have near monopolies on labor in some industries, and public sector unions have absolute monopolies on labor. Together, they directly and indirectly raise business costs in the U.S.

Fourth, our country's multiple healthcare failures cause healthcare to cost twice as much in the U.S. as in most other countries. Health insurance for a family that costs as much as 28 percent of people's earnings is a serious competitive disadvantage.

While politicians and journalists blame the loss of American jobs, technology, and enterprise on inexpensive foreign labor, the truth is that our leaders' poor policy choices and practices are the primary causes. The unfriendly fiscal, monetary, tax, regulatory, energy, and healthcare policies of the U.S. and the more business-friendly policies of other countries incentivize companies to flee our shores.

Entitlement

The rapidly growing living standards of the 1940s and 1950s made most Americans feel fortunate and the future look bright. The Social Security and Unemployment Insurance programs and generous pension plans gave people a strong sense of financial security.

Having received a green light from the Supreme Court to enact social programs, liberals convinced majorities of our federal representatives to pass a Disability Insurance program in the 1950s and the Food Stamp, Medicare, Medicaid, and Welfare programs in the 1960s. The prevailing rationale was that America was so awesome that no citizen should endure poverty.

Supporters of these programs wanted to help people, but they also wanted to increase their political power. They branded their opposition as heartless and won the day. They removed the stigma associated with public support, and they have worked hard to sign people up for these programs ever since.

The federal, state, or local level of government that could best address poverty was not a consideration. The fact that none of these programs had been piloted did not matter. Program tendencies to incentivize complacency and idleness and cost billions and trillions of dollars over time were nonissues.

Before too many years passed, the days of believing that "we must earn our own way" gave way to "I am an American; I deserve a good life," and then, "I not only deserve a good life; I have a right to a good life." Lee Kuan Yew, the founding father of Singapore and its prime minister from 1965 to 1990, understood the importance of avoiding entitlement mentalities.

In just three decades, his leadership moved Singapore from Third World to First World. It transformed a poor, decrepit, crime-ridden city into a modern, affluent, orderly city-state and perhaps the most livable city in the world. His leadership and methods underlie many of China's recent successes. Statesmen and scholars the world over consider Lee Kuan Yew to have been one of the greatest leaders of the twentieth century. Commenting on the Western approach to poverty, he stated:

> American and European governments believed that they could always afford to support the poor and the needy: widows, orphans, the old and homeless, disadvantaged minorities, unwed mothers. Their sociologists expounded the theory that hardship and failure were due not to the individual person's character, but to flaws in the economic system. So charity became "entitlement," and the stigma of living on charity disappeared. Unfortunately, welfare costs grew faster than the government's ability to raise taxes to pay for it. The political cost of tax increases is high. Governments took the easy way out by borrowing to give higher benefits to the current generation of voters and passing the costs on to the future generations who were not yet voters.[20]

Entitlements and the political power associated with them are poisonous. They negatively affect the people of every welfare state and drive ever more wealth redistribution and taxation. They destroy people's incentives to learn, work, and save. They precipitate a loss of competitiveness and an eventual relative decline in living standards.

Lest you think that I am heartless and that I do not recognize that many people need a little help, bear with me. I discuss the Winning Practices and what Lee Kuan Yew did to create a thriving population without entitlement mentalities in *Flourish: Winning Practices of Government and Enterprise*.

Consumerism and Debt

The rapidly growing standards of living of the 1940s and 1950s and the cradle-to-grave social safety net of the 1960s caused people to loosen up. It caused them to save less for the future, spend more freely, and borrow more. The days of waiting until one had money to purchase something and saving money for hardships and retirement gradually passed for large portions of the population.

Americans had for decades used credit to finance their homes, but in the 1970s they started to purchase their cars with credit and to acquire credit cards. In the 1980s, they used credit to supplement their lifestyles, financing the purchase of their back-to-school clothes, birthday gifts, holiday gifts, televisions, and furniture. In the 1990s, Americans started borrowing to purchase houses that had twice the square footage of their parents' homes.

Throughout the 1980s, 1990s, and the first seven years of the 2000s, liberals pushed hard for low-income ownership of homes. They pressed banks to lower their lending standards. They pressured Freddie Mac and Fannie Mae, federally sponsored institutions, to support more and more low-income home ownership. These efforts enabled people to purchase houses with no money down. They enabled people who had a negative net worth and just enough income to make the payments on a thirty-year mortgage to qualify for mortgages.

In the 1980s and 1990s, more and more Americans started to finance their college education. Well-intended lawmakers facilitated this practice with the federally sponsored Sallie Mae institution. Sallie Mae essentially eliminated most of the previously required qualifications for loans and offered students extremely lenient repayment terms. Now, seven in ten college students leave school with tens of thousands of dollars in student loans, and the federally sponsored loan system is rapidly becoming insolvent.

What is the net effect of all this consumerism and debt? In 1964, total U.S. public and private debt was 1.06 trillion dollars. In 2014, it increased to 61.54 trillion dollars.[21] In 1964, some 60.20 million people were employed in our country. In 2014, approximately 141.48 million people were employed.[22] This works out to $17,600 dollars of debt per employed person in 1964 and $435,000 of debt per employed person in 2014. The picture is far worse than this if we include the unfunded and underfunded commitments that federal, state, and local governments have made regarding public pensions, Social Security, Medicaid, Medicare, disability, and healthcare.

When we consume mindlessly, save little, and borrow large sums, we live today at the expense of tomorrow. We have less investment income and pay more interest. Our government receives less tax revenue and pays more interest. We invest less in infrastructure, research, and development. Our productivity and living standards stagnate. Our competitiveness declines. Our country becomes weak. Others challenge us, and we are less able to overcome our challenges. When we live today at the expense of tomorrow, we diminish our children's future.

Easy Money

Easy money occurs when a country's central bank (1) decreases the amount of reserves commercial and retail banks must hold for each dollar they lend, (2) pays commercial and retail banks artificially low rates of interest to hold their money, or (3) buys its government's debt. Easy money distorts market prices. It enables enterprises and consumers to borrow at lower interest rates and causes the prices of goods, services, and assets to increase.

It was the easy money policies of the late 1990s and early 2000s that set up the Great Recession of 2007–2009. The central bank implemented easy money policies to avoid the Y2K uncertainty and to stabilize the economy after the September 11 attacks. It continued easy money policies in the 2000s to keep the good times rolling. These policies enabled governments, enterprises, and consumers to borrow and keep on spending.

The demand for goods, services, assets, and debt does not increase at increasing rates forever either in normal or easy money environments. Eventually, governments, enterprises, and consumers slow their purchases and use of debt. Then, the prices of most things decrease.

Like a receding tide exposes the beach, falling prices expose high levels of financial institution and consumer debt. This happened when declining real estate prices exposed irresponsible levels of debt at Bear Stearns, Countrywide Financial, Fannie Mae, Freddie Mac, Goldman Sachs, Lehman Brothers, Merrill Lynch, and numerous other financial institutions in 2008. The declining asset prices decreased the value of the limited amounts of collateral the financial institutions held, woke up investors, and caused panic.

To restore order, the central bank implemented even more aggressive easy money policies than those that precipitated the asset bubbles in the first place. While an aggressive easy money policy was an appropriate response to the financial crisis, it was not appropriate to continue it for seven or eight more years. Moreover, it was not appropriate for the central bank to purchase approximately $2.5 trillion of U.S. debt between 2008 and 2014, essentially creating money out of thin air to keep interest rates for commercial and retail banks well under one-quarter percent through 2015.

While easy money can temper economic constructions, it also distorts market prices, decreases capital formation, and creates speculative bubbles. It steals purchasing power from savers and gives it to borrowers. It enables governments, enterprises, and consumers to continue the reckless borrowing and spending that causes great recessions. In short, easy money is like heroin: once a central authority starts using it, it cannot stop without causing a lot of pain and suffering.

Hubris and Nation-Building

Hubris surfaces after long periods of success. It frequently manifests itself in the children of highly successful generations, who usually are less aware of the knowledge, discipline, and hard work that success requires. They grow up comfortably and do not acquire the same insights, habits, discipline, and judgment of prior generations. They live large and develop a false sense of reality. Hubris precipitates poor judgment.

The change in the election of U.S. senators, constitutional decoupling, promiscuity, the liberalism of education, relativism, multiculturalism, nonjudgmentalism, entitlement, consumerism, excessive debt, and easy money are all manifestations of hubris. To this list, we should add nation-building.

Having had tremendous success in helping Germany and Japan rebuild after WWII and South Korea after the Korean War, George W. Bush, Dick Cheney, Donald Rumsfeld, and others believed that we could depose any government and build a better one at will. What they failed to recognize was that the Germans, Japanese, and South Koreans had as much to do with their success after WWII and the Korean War as we did. The German, Japanese, and South Koreans had a high prevalence of Winning Perspectives and Practices within their culture before our arrival.

Attempts to nation-build in Afghanistan and Iraq were doomed from the start. The Afghans and Iraqis have many values that are incompatible with ours, and they have a much lower prevalence of Winning Practices within their populations. The cost of the misguided attempts to nation-build in Afghanistan and Iraq, in terms of treasure, life, and social cohesion, have been staggering.

Immigration Failures

We have many immigration failures. We fail to control our borders and allow millions of immigrants to illegally enter our country, some of whom are terrorists, criminals, and people who carry life-threatening diseases. We flood our labor markets with immigrants, depressing wage rates and making it even harder for our citizens to find employment.

Immigrants enter our country who mean us harm and who do not know our language, do not share our values, have no prospect of employment, and will depend on public resources the rest of their lives. Desirable applicants with needed work skills wait, while our agencies deal with the thousands of illegal immigrants. Legal and illegal immigrants concentrate in Southern California and South Florida, overwhelming the schools, health services, police forces, courts, jails, and social services in these areas.

In 1965, 5 percent of the U.S. population was foreign born. In 2015, 14 percent of the population, or approximately 45 million people, were foreign born.[23] In 1965, our families were more intact, our communities were safer, and our population was fitter. Real wages were increasing faster, proportionally fewer people were unemployed, and proportionally fewer people depended on the government. For the most part, we all spoke one language, our people were more unified, and we were less indebted.

Distorted News

One of the great unifying forces in our country was the existence of three or four national media outlets and two or three newspapers in most communities. The few national and local newspapers, radio, and television options assured large general audiences. These organizations incentivized their operators to uphold national and local community standards and appeal to all Americans. If news media operators did these things, they were assured substantial audiences and revenues. If they did not, they failed.

With the advent of cable television and the Internet, the few national news organizations fragmented into numerous ones. They received revenue and large audiences only as they catered to niches, targeted their programming, and selectively reported.

While greater choice and customized services generally have merit, this was not the case with the news media. We now live in a world where most people are exposed to half of the world's realities and only receive news that aligns with their views.

Political Polarization

A country comprised of people of multiple races, religions, and ethnic groups who live, attend school, and work in different locales and have substantially different living standards is polarizing. A federal legislature where half plus one of the representatives and senators enact controversial laws is polarizing. An order where half of the population depends on social programs and the other half of the population pays for them is polarizing. Fragmented news organizations that tailor their news reports to niche markets reinforce the polarization.

The social cohesion of our citizens is probably lower than at any time in our history except for a few years during and after the Revolutionary and Civil wars. People vehemently favor the protection of the unborn or a woman's right to choose. They favor less government, free market solutions, and lower taxes, or more social programs, more regulation, and higher taxes. They favor a larger or smaller military and more or less immigration. They deny that greenhouse gas emissions are a problem or they want the government to force people to reduce their emissions.

People assume the positions that are common among their social circles. Fact-based, rational discussions are difficult. Middle ground and common sense are rare. The practice of piloting policies and projects on a small scale and thoroughly examining their effects seldom occurs.

Separation from Nature

For some one hundred years, most Americans have been separated from nature and have had a cursory exposure to science. While we might visit a park or go camping a few times a year, most of us spend most of our time in manmade habitats. We might have taken some science at school and college, but most of us do not grasp the implications of many of its findings.

We experience environments of wood, steel, concrete, and glass located on lawns and pavement, and we have little experience with large populations of plants and animals, savannahs, woodlands, jungles, deserts, frozen tundra, and oceans. This is most unfortunate, as we do not sense our dependence upon our planet—its rhythms, climate, atmosphere, fresh water, soils, ecosystems, plants, and animals. We do not appreciate the cycle of life—the coevolution of predators and prey and the importance of fitness. We do not understand that we must perform and have offspring like all plants and animals, or we, our culture, and our progeny perish. We do not grasp the vulnerability of individuals and the strength of families and communities. We do not understand what we can cause in one lifetime and what takes several generations to change. Most people's separation from nature and limited understanding of science are unfortunate because wisdom comes from an accurate understanding of them.

Our technology creates an illusion that we are apart from nature, but we are not. We are very much a part of nature and must align our perspectives and practices with it. Affluence and technology give a license to live foolishly and contrary to nature for a while, but eventually our health, fitness, wellbeing, and success depend upon the alignment of our actions with the universe and its processes, life and its processes, and human nature.

Losing Our Way

Inclusion Failures
The Change in the Election of U.S. Senators
Presidential Constitutional Failings
Supreme Court Constitutional Failings

Special Interest Government
Less Faith-Community Relevance
Less Integrity, Responsibility, and Civility
Promiscuity and the Decline of Marriage

Poorly Parented Children
Unionization of Education
Liberalization of Education
Social Justice Missteps

Relativism, Nonjudgmentalism, and Multiculturalism
Declining Discipline, Poor Habits, and Less Learning
Oligopoly and Monopoly
Offshoring

Entitlement
Consumerism and Debt
Easy Money
Hubris and Nation-Building

Immigration Failures
Distorted News
Political Polarization
Separation from Nature

CHAPTER 2

Winning Perspectives

Winning Perspectives come to us from an understanding of the evolution of the universe, life, and culture. They help us distinguish Winning Practices from a murky sea of unlimited possibilities.

Singapore, Switzerland, and the United States

Of all the countries that I have visited and studied in the world, Singapore and Switzerland seem to thrive the most. Larger portions of their populations utilize greater numbers of Winning Perspectives and Practices than the other countries with which I am familiar.

In 2009 and 2010, when I was running for Congress, our citizens were debating healthcare. From prior experience with the research of Regina Herzlinger, a professor at the Harvard Business School and author of several books on healthcare, and from my travels, I knew that Switzerland had one of the best healthcare systems in the world. At a CEO Harvard Presidents' Seminar, Professor Herzlinger indicated that consumers, healthcare providers, and insurers in Switzerland all rated the Swiss healthcare system higher than the same stakeholder groups in other countries rated their systems. After studying Switzerland's health-care system and understanding its merits firsthand, I started talking about it on the campaign trail.

People's reactions surprised and saddened me. Most people either liked our current system at the time or President Obama's approach. Few cared to learn about Switzerland's consumer-driven system and how we might more prudently offer universal healthcare.

Figure 4: Singapore, Switzerland, and the United States

	Singapore	Switzerland	USA
Country Characteristics			
Natural Resources	None	Few	Abundant
Major Languages	4	4	2
Population (millions)	6	8	320
Freedom & Opportunity			
Freedom Index Score (lower is freer)	43rd	2nd	20th
Economic Freedom Rank (lower is freer)	2nd	4th	16th
Youth Unemployment in 2015 (ages 15-24)	7.0%	8.3%	13.4%
Unemployment Rate in 2015	2.0%	3.3%	5.2%
Home Ownership Rate	90%	45%	65%
Quality of Government			
Country Corruption Rank (lower is less corrupt)	7th	5th	17th
Homicides (per 100,000 people)	0.2	0.6	4.7
Incarceration Rate (per 100,000 people)	220	85	700
Public Debt Per Employed Person	$60,000	$32,000	$129,000
Foreign Exchange and Gold Reserves Per Capita	$45,800	$73,000	$400
Family Function			
Adolescent Fertility Rate (births/1,000 women ages 15-19)	4	4	30
Divorces to Marriages Per Year	28%	51%	53%
Population Replenishment, (> 2.1 births / woman → growth)	1.3	1.5	1.9
Individual Well-Being			
Infant Mortality Rate	2.2%	3.5%	5.7%
Obesity Rate	7%	18%	33%
Portion of the Population with Health Insurance	100%	100%	88%
Health Expenditures as a Percent of GNP	5%	12%	17%
Life Expectancy at Birth (years)	82	83	79
Education			
Portion of the Population Completing High School	67%	86%	89%
Portion of Population Completing ≥ 2 yrs. of College	47%	37%	43%
Researchers (per million citizens)	6300	5000	3840
Competitiveness and Income			
Tax Rate on Commercial Profits	18%	29%	44%
GDP Per Capita 2015	$85,300	$58,600	$55,800
GDP Increase Over 55 Years	199x	33x	19x
Sustainability			
CO_2 Emissions Per Capita (metric tons)	2.7	5.0	17.5
Mammal Species Threatened	10	2	35

One of the challenges of success, as I mentioned in the last chapter, is that it often leads to hubris, closed-mindedness, and poor choices. Individuals, organizations, and countries that are successful and remain successful over time avoid hubris and closed-mindedness. They continuously benchmark and learn from others.

Figure 4 provides some comparison of life in Singapore, Switzerland, and the United States. After reviewing it, I think most people will agree that we can learn many things from Singapore, Switzerland, and such comparisons.

Country Characteristics

Life in Singapore and Switzerland is extremely desirable. This is amazing given both countries have little developable real estate and few natural resources. More amazing is that Singapore lacked its own water supply and was as poor as Haiti in the 1960s, and it now has the sixth highest per-capita income in the world.

Like our country, Singapore and Switzerland are multicultural. The Asian city-state of Singapore is primarily made up of Chinese, Malays, and Indians who speak English, Mandarin, Malay, or Tamil. Its principal religions include Buddhism, Islam, Hinduism, and Christianity. The small European country of Switzerland is primarily made up of people with German, French, Italian, and Romansh heritages. Each of these groups speaks its own language, and most Swiss historically are either Roman Catholic or Protestant.

For decades, the Chinese dominated the Malays and Indians in Singapore, and the three groups did not get along well. In the 1960s, Singapore had racial riots break out. In Europe, the Germans, Italians, French, Catholics, and Protestants did not get along well for centuries. Today though, the Singaporeans and the Swiss make national cohesiveness a national priority, work at it, and enjoy enviable cultural harmony.

While Singapore's and Switzerland's populations are only 6 million and 8 million people relative to the 320 million people in the U.S., their smaller size is not the cause of their success.[24] Rather, their success is a function of their leadership and the high prevalence of Winning Perspectives and Practices within their populations. Leadership, culture, and Winning Perspectives and Practices are scalable.

Freedom and Opportunity

In 2015, Singapore, Switzerland, and the United States ranked 43rd, 2nd, and 20th, respectively, on the Cato Institute's Freedom Index, and second, fourth, and sixteenth on their Economic Freedom Index.[25] While Singapore scores low on the overall Freedom Index relative to Switzerland and the U.S., it has been steadily improving its scores as the vestiges of Lee Kuan Yew's dictatorship recede. Singapore and Switzerland both score much better than the U.S. on the Economic Freedom Index.

Youth unemployment runs 7.0, 8.6, and 13.4 percent in Singapore, Switzerland, and the U.S., respectively while overall unemployment runs 2.0, 3.3, and 5.2 percent in the three countries.[26] Home ownership rates are 90 percent in Singapore, 45 percent in Switzerland, and 65 percent in the U.S.[27]

Singapore's home ownership rate, the highest in the world, is stunning. The Winning Practices of low tax rates and compulsory savings are responsible. These practices yield far more benefits to the population than the high income tax rates, low savings rates, and wasteful government spending practices of Western countries. When people own their homes, they steadily build equity as they age. They feel secure and good about themselves. They develop a tremendous pride in their neighborhoods and country. The Winning Practices of low tax rates and compulsory savings are completely untried in the West. I discuss them in more detail in *Flourish: Winning Practives of Government and Enterprise*.

Quality of Government

In the 1950s, the U.S. was considered one of the least corrupt and Singapore one of the most corrupt countries in the world. Now, according to Transparency International, Singapore and Switzerland have substantially less corruption than the U.S.

I would guess that most fifty and older U.S. citizens, like me, have noticed throughout their lives the increasing dishonesty and lawlessness in our country. My parents and many other parents felt no need to regularly lock their homes or cars when I was young, and most students had no need of lockers in school. When public officials were caught lying or breaking the law, they resigned from office and often went to jail. Such integrity is rarer today, and our loss of it is not something we should accept, as corruption lowers living standards and negatively affects our well-being.

The Western elite has nothing but disdain for Singapore's rule of law—more particularly, its use of fines and caning for noncriminal offenses and capital punishment for drug dealers instead of prison sentences for these offenses. How foolish! Unlike many Americans, Singaporeans universally live in safe neighborhoods. They do not fear crime because it is so rare in Singapore. Homicides average 0.2, 0.6, and 4.7 per 100,000 citizens in Singapore, Switzerland, and the U.S., respectively.[29] You are twenty-four times more likely to be murdered in the U.S. than in Singapore, and for many people living in U.S. cities, the murder rate is several hundred times higher in U.S. than Singapore. The U.S. incarcerates people at more than three times the rate of Singapore and more than eight times the rate of Switzerland.[30] The rule of law in Singapore not only protects people, but it deters crime! It keeps families safe and together. It provides an environment for people to flourish!

Singapore and Switzerland both have had to coexist with powerful, hostile neighbors. While no one desires such neighbors, they can be a blessing in disguise when countries avoid conflicts with them and respond wisely to them. Powerful, hostile neighbors unify a country and sometimes indirectly increase the prevalence of Winning Perspectives and Practices within the population by causing it to conscript young males into the military and better enculturate them.

Smaller, vulnerable countries take their defenses seriously. Singapore and Switzerland both do this. Men must serve in the military or do public service, and through such service, they become more disciplined. They acquire additional organizational, vocational, and intercultural skills. They learn to lead and follow at an early age, and they learn to live and work with all types of people. They develop a love for their country and greater social cohesiveness.

Being small relative to other countries also causes the Singaporeans and the Swiss to avoid undertaking foolish nation-building activities in other countries. While highly selective attempts to nation-build sometimes pay dividends, they often waste lives and resources.

Singapore and Switzerland have had more effective governments than the U.S. The $60,000, $32,000, and $129,000 of public debt per employed person and the $45,800, $73,000, and $400 of respective foreign exchange and gold reserves per person are evidence of this. Unlike the U.S., Singapore and Switzerland maintain balanced budgets.[31] They do not run deficits year after year, and their citizens form more of the capital that their economies require.

The Swiss also can check their lawmakers. Many new laws require a national referendum for approval, and as few as fifty thousand Swiss citizens may force a referendum on any new federal law. Swiss parliament members serve part time and favor special interests much less than our U.S. Senators and Congressional Representatives.

Family Function

Other striking comparisons among the three countries relate to family. Births per one thousand women ages fifteen to nineteen are 4, 4, and 30 respectively in Singapore, Switzerland, and the U.S.[32] This means that teenage pregnancy is seven to eight times more prevalent in the U.S. than in Singapore and Switzerland.

Divorces to marriages per year are 28 percent in Singapore, 51 percent in Switzerland, and 53 percent in the U.S.[33] My experience in these countries and knowledge of them suggest that the more traditional family-related practices of Singapore and the greater opportunities for women and modern family arrangements in Switzerland and the U.S. account for some of the difference in the divorce rates between Singapore and Western countries.

All three countries have birth rates that will not sustain their populations and cultures. Singapore's and Switzerland's are the lowest.[34] Each country must significantly raise its birth rate to 2.1 births per woman or accept more immigrants to sustain its population.

Individual Well-being

Infant mortality is 2.2, 3.5, and 5.7 percent in Singapore, Switzerland, and the U.S., respectively.[35] Seven percent of the population is obese in Singapore, 18 percent in Switzerland, and, sadly, 33 percent in the U.S.[36] Obesity is a primary cause of diabetes, heart disease, cancer, premature death, and large medical bills. How can a people flourish when more than one-third of its population is obese?

In Singapore and Switzerland, 100 percent of the population is covered by health insurance. In the U.S., even after the Affordable Care Act, 88 percent of the population is covered.[37] Health expenditures as a percent of gross domestic product per capita (GDP) in Singapore, Switzerland, and the U.S. are 5, 12, and 17 percent, respectively.[38] Like Swiss healthcare, Singaporean healthcare is consumer-driven, of high quality, and a great value. In Singapore, life expectancy for men and women is eighty-two years, in Switzerland, eighty-three years, and in the U.S, seventy-nine years.[39] Singaporeans and Swiss spend less on healthcare and live longer than Americans because they are fitter.

Education

Comparing education across the three countries reveals that while the U.S. once led the world in education, it has lost its edge in the last twenty years and the U.S. still graduates a larger proportion of its population from high school, but it no longer graduates a larger proportion from college. The higher U.S. high school graduation rate may be misleading in the sense that many of our schools allow our students to graduate without mastering the material.[40] Singapore, Switzerland, and many other countries have larger portions of their populations engaged in research.[41]

Competitiveness and Income

The U.S. tax on corporate profits of 44 percent is much higher than the rate of most other nations. Singapore's rate is 18 percent, and Switzerland's rate is 29 percent.[42] High corporate tax rates cause businesses to locate and take profits in other countries. They reduce the availability of good jobs, lower people's wages, and decrease tax revenues.

One can see the results of Winning Perspectives and Practices through the change in living standards over time. The GDP per capita is $85,300, $58,600, and $55,800 in Singapore, Switzerland, and the U.S., respectively.[43] In the last fifty-four years, living standards have increased 199 times in Singapore, 33 times in Switzerland, and only 19 times in the U.S.[44] The greater prevalence of Winning Perspectives and Practices in Singapore and Switzerland makes a real difference over time.

Sustainability

The U.S. pours far more climate-altering greenhouse gases into the atmosphere per capita than do Singapore and Switzerland. Currently, we emit an estimated 17.5 tons of CO_2 per person, while the Singaporeans and Swiss emit only 2.7 and 5.0 tons per person, respectively.[45] Currently, the populations of Singapore, Switzerland, and the U.S. threaten ten, two, and thirty-five mammalian species, respectively.[46]

Winning Perspectives

Visiting and studying other countries gives us tremendous perspective. It helps us understand that our ways of doing things are not the only ways. Yet, such comparisons are only advantageous as they surface practices that work. As someone who is part farmer, entrepreneur, scientist, and investor, I am unusually realistic and practical. What matters to me is not what sounds good but what works! Millions of acres of plants, millions of animals, thousands of enterprises, and millions of jobs depend on the accurate diagnosis of problems and realistic assessment of potential solutions.

Most successful people, organizations, and governments ground their thoughts, decisions, and actions in reality. They base them on insights for which there is evidence. They learn from accomplished mentors. They test hypotheses. They pilot new approaches on a small scale before committing resources on a large scale.

People who accomplish a lot have little patience with those who purposely distort reality or peddle fanciful and unproven theories and approaches. They have little patience with people who advocate something without having experience or evidence of its effectiveness.

Just because some ideas sound good does not mean that they will work. Just because someone told us something was true when we were young does not make it so. People mean well, but they repeat what they are told or tell us what we want to hear, whether it is true or false. We must be cautious about what we accept as true, as distortions of reality lead to poor decisions that yield streams of unintended adverse effects.

Under the leadership of Jack Welch, General Electric increased in market value forty times in just twenty years.[47] Welch attributes much of his success and General Electric's success under his leadership to his mother's relentless emphasis on facing reality. He writes:

> The insights she drilled into me never faded. She always insisted on facing the facts of a situation. One of her favorite expressions was "Don't kid yourself. That's the way it is."[48]

I, too, am interested in reality, what works, and the perspectives and practices that enable us to thrive. Fashion, ideals, and political correctness do not interest me, as fashions are temporary, ideals are imagined states of perfection, and political correctness exists to further someone's political agenda. Reality is as it is, and not as we wish it to be! Thus, it is with the highest regard for evidence-based, accurate views of reality that I have assembled the eight Winning Perspectives found in this book: Truth, Causality, Scale, Evolution, Fitness, Human Nature, Periodic Disaster, and Eco-Dependency.

Winning Perspectives—*accurate perceptions of reality and conditions of existence. Substantial evidence exists for them. They further our effectiveness and help us identify Winning Practices.*

CHAPTER 3

Truth

The truth is incontrovertible. Malice may attack it, ignorance may deride it, but in the end, there it is.[49]

–Winston Churchill

The first of the eight Winning Perspectives is Truth. The potency of Winning Perspectives and Practices rests on their "truth," their approximation of reality and alignment with it.

Discerning truth requires perspective, thought, and hard work. Often, things are not what they seem. While the sun appears to move across the horizon, we now know it is the spin of the Earth and movement of our horizon that causes the illusion. Similarly, the Earth seems flat even though it is spherical. Only after perceptive and courageous mariners sailed around large portions of the world did we accept this reality.

Some discoveries of truth require a lot of collaboration and technology. For example, we thought a creator formed the universe for thousands of years. Not until scientists worked out the sequence of events and the conditions for them to occur did we realize that the universe self-assembles. Scientists and technicians could not have gathered this knowledge without hundreds of years of disciplined inquiry and thousands of technological advances. Telescopes, microscopes, computers, particle accelerators, and space probes contributed mightily to our current understanding.

Discerning truth is also difficult because mental filters distort our perceptions. As the maxim states, "We do not see things as they are; we see things as we are." If we lived in the wilderness and learned at a young age that Native Americans were heathen murderers, we would hide from them and probably shoot those who strayed onto our property. We would completely miss the reality that the early Native Americans were people who loved their children, enjoyed their families and communities, and just wanted to retain their lands and live their lives.

How do we come to acquire mental filters that distort our perceptions? We are born into groups that teach them to us. The views that we learn, especially when young, burrow into our subconscious, be they conservative, liberal, Jewish, Christian, Muslim, atheist, or other. They become the lenses through which we see the world.

Early in our lives, we are open to others' views, particularly those of the people we trust and those who have authority over us, such as our parents, older siblings, teachers, and coaches. As we strive to become independent from our parents, the views of our peers influence us. In a sense, our views are always becoming a little more like the views of those with whom we spend the most time.

Sometime in our midtwenties, when our routines and the people with whom we spend the most time stabilize, our views of the world solidify. We are open to information that reinforces our views and closed to information that challenges them. These groupthink tendencies create social cohesion and aid survival. We recognize these tendencies as outsiders of groups, but we do not notice them as insiders. Objectivity and social cohesion conflict with one another.

Conservatives view government as inefficient, wasteful, and restrictive. They oppose increasing the scale and scope of it. On the other hand, liberals see government as a helpful tool to eliminate prejudice and inequality. They support the expansion of it. Many Christians see human life starting at conception, and many non-Christians see it starting after some fetal development. Americans see terrorist acts as barbaric. Muslim extremists see the acts as heroic advancements of Allah's will. In each case, people see the world through the lens of those with whom they most closely affiliate.

Along with groupthink, self-interest colors our perceptions. We see events as it is in our interests to see them. If we collide with a car at a four-way stop, most people will tend to blame the other driver. If one of our children is involved in a fight, most of us will fault the other child, unless our child has a history of fighting. When we propose an idea, plan, or program, we have an interest in its success. If people's reactions are mixed to our idea, we register their praise more than their criticism. As inventor extraordinaire Thomas Edison wrote:

> If we bother with facts at all, we hunt like bird dogs after the facts that bolster up what we already think—and ignore all the others! We want only the facts that justify our acts—the facts that fit in conveniently with [our] wishful-thinking and justify our preconceived prejudices![50]

Grasping truth is hard because we often do not communicate it. We all want to appear unselfish and noble. We want others to see us in a positive light, so we mask our true intentions and create narratives. We tell others what we want them to hear or what they want to hear.

Perceptive children tell their parents what they want to hear. Leaders and politicians treat their constituents, and subordinates treat their superiors in the same manner. Unless we are infused with a strong truth-telling ethic, telling the truth when we have something to hide or hurtful to say stresses us while telling others what they want to hear relaxes us.

Though it is rare, truth is ever so important. It depicts reality and the cause and effect relationships. It helps us act in ways that yield streams of positive effects, while deception causes us to act in ways that yield streams of negative effects. Truth furthers freedom, fitness, and decency, while deception furthers tyranny, weakness, and injustice. Except when we deal with those who mean us harm, life goes better when we speak truthfully and vanquish deception. Carl Sagan wrote:

> The truth may be puzzling. It may take some work to grapple with. It may be counterintuitive. It may contradict deeply held prejudices. It may not be consonant with what we desperately want to be true. But our preferences do not determine what's true.[51]

Reading, traveling, education, experience, and others' viewpoints help us to recognize our mental filters and free ourselves from them. Usually we do not grasp reality until we experience it from several vantage points. Children and professional magicians see magic differently. Children see the illusion. Magicians see the artistry and deceptions. Both see the performances, but magicians see them with more understanding. Experienced professionals see detail in their areas of expertise more accurately. People who consult experts, solicit different points of view, and conduct experiments improve their perception of reality.

Because so much works against our perception and conveyance of truth, and because truth is so essential to our effectiveness, we must appreciate those who try to discern and express truth. Leaders, parents, and teachers especially should expect others to be truthful, and they should reward truthful behavior. Similarly, we all should reward truthfulness, penalize lying, and relieve liars of their responsibilities.

Leaders, authorities, famous people, and those engaged in science, research, and teaching have a special responsibility to convey accurate and balanced views, as their views affect many other people. Imagine the harm done to people were a doctor to tell them that smoking poses no risk; or the harm done to students when adults tell them that they are stupid. Think about the harm done to our country when journalists do not report unconstitutional and unlawful acts of our leaders and representatives.

I discuss the scientific method and its quest to describe reality accurately in a subsequent book, *Flourish: Winning Practices of Families and Education.* Even the scientific method is not foolproof, though. Sometimes truth eludes scientists for decades.

The twentieth-century qualification of Newton's laws of motion provides one of the best examples of this and underscores the importance of avoiding certitude. Every related experiment confirmed Newton's laws of motion for over two hundred years. But Einstein discovered that the laws only provide approximations of reality at familiar scales and are incorrect at large and small scales.

With method, discipline, and persistence, we approximate truth, but we can never be certain that we have captured it. We must always remain open to the possibility that more accurate depictions exist. Carl Sagan wrote:

> Humans may crave absolute certainty; they may aspire to it; they may pretend, as partisans of certain religions do, to have attained it. But the history of science—by far the most successful claim to knowledge accessible to humans—teaches that the most we can hope for is successive improvement in our understanding.[52]

Reality is as it is. The workings of the universe and life are as they are. Truth accurately depicts them. We must work hard to understand reality and not run from it. We may avoid truth, but we cannot avoid reality or the workings of the universe. We can fight for our perspectives and understanding of truth, but we must not believe they are truth.

Truth—*accurate approximations of reality, natural processes, and events.*

CHAPTER 4

Causality

Behind every event is one or more causes.

We have poorly understood the cause and effect nature of the universe for most of history, as most causes are invisible to us. For thousands of years, we thought capricious acts of gods, God, wizards, and witches caused diseases, pestilence, and famine. Not until Robert Hooke and others had the benefit of the microscope did we learn that bacteria cause many diseases. Not until we understood the gestation cycles of insects did we discover the cause of pestilence. Only when we learned of the effects that massive volcanic eruptions had on Earth's temperatures did we recognize that they were one of the major causes of famine.

Without telescopes, microscopes, and other sensory aids, most of the universe and natural processes are imperceptible to us. Cosmic structure and distances, the fusion of the elements, and DNA's orchestration of life and cell division are undetectable. Without sensory aids, understanding the galaxies, stars, and planets and the multibillion-year sequence of events that created them is impossible. Without the fossil record, careful observation, and imagination, the evolution of life and the innumerable small changes that occur over thousands of generations are imperceptible.

It took thousands of scientists hundreds of years to expose the sequence of cause and effects that shaped the universe and life over the last 13.7 billion years. Although scientists have numerous details to work out, they understand the major events. While the events before the big bang, the first fraction of a second of the big bang, and the most fundamental forms of matter and energy remain mysteries, there is every reason to believe that the last two mysteries will give way as scientists continue to subject them to scientific inquiry.

Understanding that there are one or more causes for every event is a giant step forward for people. Ceasing to attribute events to gods, God, wizards, witches, bad luck, and others' ill intentions, and knowing the real causes improves our quality of life.

I learned quickly on the farm and in business that it is crucial to understand the cause or causes of problems. When we do not find the cause or causes of a problem, we often only address the symptoms of it. While alleviating the symptoms of a problem may make us feel better, it does not solve the problem. The problem remains and grows.

Consider the challenge of providing clean drinking water to a community, where the only adequate source of water is a lake high in phosphates and nitrates. The municipality has two choices: require land-owners to put in vegetation buffers and retention ponds around the lake to manage runoff from their properties, or treat the water to reduce the phosphates and nitrates to acceptable levels. The first approach has a high initial cost, eliminates the contamination, and forever solves the problem. The second approach has a low initial cost, high ongoing costs, and does not eliminate the underlying problem. Which is the better solution? While the answer to this question depends on the severity of the adverse effects and the costs and benefits of the alternative approaches over time, addressing the causes of a problem and eliminating them is usually superior to treating its symptoms.

Fallacy, Correlation, Necessity, and Sufficiency

When thinking about causes and their effects, understanding the concepts of fallacy, correlation, necessity, and sufficiency is helpful.

A **Fallacy** is the incorrect attribution of cause to effect.

"You will catch a cold if you go outside with wet hair" is a fallacy. It is a fallacy because viruses cause colds, not wet hair. "Government may lower the cost of healthcare by setting the prices for it" is a fallacy, as price fixing does nothing to lower the providers' cost of delivering healthcare services. It merely decreases the number of providers and increases the time people wait for the services offered by the remaining lower cost and/or poorer quality providers. Fallacies are far more common than we realize. They occur where resources are scarce, people are ignorant, and superstition prevails, and they frequently occur in bureaucracies where people spend others' money and have little accountability.

Correlation is the simultaneous occurrence of two events.

Correlation does not imply causation. It implies coincidence. Correlations may be random, causal, or joint products of some event. One of the most common fallacies is to believe a correlation between two events implies a causal relationship.

Consider a hypothetical health study that finds a correlation between eating organic foods and a lower incidence of colds. Does the correlation mean that eating organic foods lowers the incidence of colds? No, the correlation does not tell us this. The association of eating organic foods and fewer colds only indicates that the two events are coincident. The correlation could result from the phenomenon that people eating organic foods have fewer children and therefore have less exposure to cold viruses. If this were the case, eating organic foods would coincide with having fewer colds, but it would not lower incidences of colds, as less exposure to children is what causes fewer colds.

Logicians and scientists distinguish the causes or conditions related to an event as contributory, necessary, or sufficient.

A Contributory Condition is a circumstance that plays a role in producing an effect.

A Necessary Condition is a circumstance that must be present to produce an effect.

Sufficient Conditions are the complete set of circumstances that must be present to produce an effect.

Regular exercise is a contributory condition of good health. It furthers good health but does not assure it. Some people have good health with or without it. Regular training is a necessary condition of winning a marathon. Entrants do not win marathons without it, but it alone does not assure victory. Running full speed into a concrete wall is a sufficient condition to harm oneself. The act alone guarantees harm.

Of these three types of conditions, sufficiency is the most interesting. Sufficiency refers to the set of conditions that must be present to produce an effect. Knowing the set is powerful. The conditions for sufficiency, like most cause and effect relationships, are usually invisible and difficult to determine, but we may discover them with careful observation and experimentation. Science excels in determining the sufficient conditions for events. Consider a simplified summary of what scientists have learned about our universe by way of observation, experimentation, and understanding the sufficient conditions of natural processes.

In the fractions of a second after the start of the universe, elementary subatomic particles formed. As the universe cooled, the motion and density of these particles became just right to cause the formation of the nuclei of simple atoms, like hydrogen, helium, and deuterium. As the universe cooled some more, the motion and density of these nuclei and free electrons became just right to cause the formation of the simple atoms themselves. As the universe continued to cool, the slower motion and greater densities of these simple atoms caused them to aggregate.

The aggregation of atoms creates gravity, pressure, and heat. Where enough hydrogen, helium, and deuterium aggregate, gravity creates temperatures of a billion degrees Kelvin, simple atoms fuse, and stars ignite. Two hydrogen protons form a deuterium nucleus and eject a positron and neutrino in the process. Large stars fuse the deuterium nuclei and heavier nuclei into all the elements on the periodic table up to iron.

Then, as the largest of these stars exhaust their supplies of these lighter elements, they collapse and explode, creating pressures and temperatures that fuse the heavier elements.

Some of the exploded debris assembles into collections of atoms that share electrons or molecules. One carbon and two oxygen atoms assemble into carbon dioxide. One nitrogen and three hydrogen atoms form ammonia. One oxygen and two hydrogen atoms form water.

The debris made up of light elements, heavy elements, and molecules coalesce into planets, asteroids, comets, and new stars. Comets of ice bombard planets, and liquids pool and evaporate. Planetary atmospheres and seas form. With the right combination of gases, liquids, temperature, and molecules, some of the molecules assemble into nucleotides and amino acids. Scientists can replicate the conditions for nucleotide and amino acid self-assembly in test tubes.

Currently, scientists are trying to determine the sufficient conditions for basic proteins to self-assemble into RNA. These conditions may have existed near alkaline vents deep within the seas some 3.8 billion years ago. If this was the case, the basic proteins and RNA most likely formed DNA and eventually one or more cells. One or more of the cells divided and the daughter cells divided again. Then, the DNA in the cells and natural selection orchestrated the formation of every cell, plant, and animal. Evidence for this possibility mounts with each passing year, as scientists gradually determine the sufficient conditions and their existence during each step of the process.

The Inanimate and Animate Worlds

Not long ago, we did not know about these conditions, processes, and events. They occurred on such a small scale, so far away, and sometimes so slowly that we did not perceive them. We attributed them to the gods or God. Knowing the sufficient conditions of an effect or event is ever more helpful.

Just as things happen at the atomic and cellular levels given the right conditions, so they happen at the organism and superorganism levels. The only difference is that higher animals inject some unpredictability into events. They make choices.

For example, usually when someone is mean to us, we reciprocate meanness if we are strong, and we flee if we are weak. Given our relative strength, there is a direct relationship between people's treatment of us and our responses. Sometimes we may circumvent the instinctual response to retaliate or flee, and respond with kindness. This is not a natural response, but a choice. Sufficient conditions for an event at the atomic and cellular levels are much more straightforward than those related to human events.

"We reap as we sow"—a reality that we receive in accordance to what we do—is a causality that generally holds. Others compensate us as we work. Others assist us as we assist them, and others harm us as we harm them. While we may not always receive our due in the short term, we frequently do in the long term.

The causality perspective teaches us that events are not arbitrary. When conditions are just right or sufficient, things happen. Simple elements assemble into heavier elements, combinations of elements assemble into molecules, some molecules assemble into amino acids, amino acids assemble into proteins, and proteins assemble into RNA, DNA, and cells. Cells divide, differentiate, and form multicellular life forms. And it just so happens that the sufficient conditions for these processes and events occur innumerable times each day either in the stars or on Earth.

Our world is comprehensible. The cause and effect relationships are predictable at the atomic and cellular levels and only slightly less predictable at the human level. Our beliefs, prayers, and preferences do not alter these causal relationships. They may affect our behavior and accordingly people's responses to us, but they do not change causal relationships. As historians, philosophers, and authors Will and Ariel Durant wrote in their eleven-volume *The Story of Civilization*:

> In the end, nothing is lost. Every event, for good or evil, has effects forever.[53]

The invisible nature of causal relationships blinds us to the effects of many of our actions. Mentors, experts, and science, especially when we are young, help us expose the long-term effects of our actions and act more prudently. Herein is a perspective and practice that all children should learn.

The thirty-six Winning Practices that I discuss in the *Flourish* series do not describe all the sufficient conditions for people to thrive, but they describe many of them. Hopefully, my attempt to delineate some of the most important ones will encourage others to describe the sufficient conditions for desired outcomes in other aspects of human life.

Causality—the reality that every effect has one or more causes.

CHAPTER 5

Scale

Fleeting specs of dust are we—transient and minute relative to the age and scope of the universe.

Our understanding of the universe, the composition of matter, and time has expanded so much the last five hundred years. Five hundred years ago, we understood distances as small as the thickness of a human hair or about 10^{-4} meters, and distances as great as a thirty-day horseback ride or about 10^4 meters. Today, we understand distances as small as one Planck length, or about 10^{-35} meters, and as large as our universe of about 10^{27} meters.

Just a few centuries ago, we understood masses as small as a mosquito or 10^{-6} kilograms, and as large as an oceangoing ship, or some 10^5 kilograms. Today, we understand masses as small as an electron of 10^{-32} kilograms and as large as a galaxy of 10^{42} kilograms.

Five hundred years ago, we had a sense of one hundred human generations, or two thousand years. Today we think in terms of millions of human generations and billions of years. Three figures that follow, Figure 5: Small and Large Distances, Figure 6: Small and Large Masses, and Figure 7: Evolution of the Universe and Life Timeline, delineate the scale of our current perspectives.

As our understanding of the scale of distance, mass, and time expands, so does our understanding of our place in the universe. Five hundred years ago, we thought the Earth was flat and God created everything for our benefit. We thought we had dominion over other animals and life forms. Now we understand that we live in one of the billions of galaxies, orbit around one of more than a billion stars in our galaxy, and live on one of the billions of potentially hospitable planets in the universe. We realize that all earthly life forms descend from a common life form, we are the products of over three billion years of natural selection, and we may become a dead leaf on the evolutionary tree, or a branch to hundreds, thousands, or even millions of generations of life.

Our view of the universe and life has changed so much in just twenty generations. Our universe seems endlessly divisible and expansive! The universe and life defy and dazzle our imaginations. They are simple, complex, and wondrous! As naturalist and Pulitzer Prize winner Annie Dillard writes:

> After the one extravagant gesture of creation in the first place, the universe has continued to deal exclusively in extravagances, flinging intricacies and colossi down eons of emptiness, heaping profusions on profligacies with ever-fresh vigor. The whole show has been on fire from the word go. I come down to the water to cool my eyes. But everywhere I look I see fire; that which isn't flint is tinder, and the whole world sparks and flames.[54]

Scale—*understanding that the magnitudes of distance, mass, and time in the universe are very different from those we experience every day. It humbles us and helps us realistically grasp our place in the universe.*

Figure 5: Small and Large Distances

English Description (Meters)	Metric Name	Number (Meters)	Scientific Notation (Meters)
Planck Length	0.16 trillionth, trillionth, trillionth		0.000,000,000,000,000,000,000,000,000,000,000,016	1.6×10^{-35}
Electron Diameter	5.6 millionth billionths	5.6 femtometers	0.000,000,000,000,0056	5.6×10^{-15}
Hydrogen Diameter	5.0 trillionths	5.0 picometers	0.000,000,000,005	5.0×10^{-12}
Smallest Transistor Gate	2.5 billionths	2.5 nanometers	0.000,000,0025	2.5×10^{-9}
Red Blood Cell Diameter	7.0 millionths	7.0 micrometers	0.000,007	7.0×10^{-6}
Human Hair Diameter	0.1 thousandths	0.1 millimeters	0.000,1	0.1×10^{-3}
Moon's Diameter	3.5 million	3.5 megameters	3,500,000	3.5×10^{6}
Earth's Diameter	12.8 thousand	12.8 megameters	12,800,000	12.8×10^{7}
Sun's Diameter	1.4 billion	1.4 gigameters	1,400,000,000	1.4×10^{9}
Earth to the Sun	150.0 billion	150.0 gigameters	150,000,000,000	150.0×10^{9}
Sun to Pluto	5.9 trillion	5.9 terameters	5,900,000,000,000	5.9×10^{12}
One Light Year	9.5 quadrillion	9.5 petameters	9,500,000,000,000,000	9.5×10^{15}
Earth to Proxima Centauri	39.9 quadrillion	39.9 petameters	39,900,000,000,000,000	39.9×10^{15}
Milky Way Diameter	1.0 billion trillion	1.0 zeptometers	1,000,000,000,000,000, 000,000	1.0×10^{21}
Universe Diameter	920.0 trillion trillion	920.0 yottameters	920,000,000,000,000,000,000,000,000	920.0×10^{25}

"Orders of Magnitude," Wikipedia,
http://en.wikipedia.org/wiki/Orders_of_magnitude_(length)

Figure 6: Small and Large Masses

	English Description	Metric Name	Number	Scientific Notation
Electron	0.9 thousandth trillionth trillionths		0.000,000,000,000,000,000,000,000,0009	0.9×10^{-27}
Hydrogen Atom	1.7 trillionth trillionths	1.7 yoctograms	0.000,000,000,000,000,000,000,0017	1.7×10^{-24}
Small Protein	55.0 billionth trillionths	55.0 zeptograms	0.000,000,000,000,000,000,000, 055	55.0×10^{-21}
Human Sperm Cell	22.0 trillionths	22.0 picograms	0.000,000,000,022	22.0×10^{-12}
Average Human Cell	1.0 billionths	1.0 nanograms	0.000,000,001	1.0×10^{-9}
Human Ovum	3.6 millionths	3.6 micrograms	0.000,0036	3.6×10^{-6}
Mosquito	2.5 thousandths	2.5 milligrams	0.025	2.5×10^{-3}
Blue Whale	200.0 million	200.0 megagrams	200,000,000	200.0×10^{6}
Human Population	400.0 trillion	400.0 teragrams	400,000,000,000,000	400×10^{12}
Moon	73.0 trillion trillion	73.0 yottagrams	73,000,000,000,000,000,000,000,000	73×10^{24}
Earth	6.0 trillion quadrillion		6,000,000,000,000,000,000,000,000,000	6.0×10^{27}
Sun	2.0 billion trillion trillion		2,000,000,000,000,000,000,000,000,000,000,000	2.0×10^{33}
Milky Way Black Hole	8.0 trillion trillion quadrillion			8.0×10^{39}
Milky Way Galaxy	1.2 billion trillion trillion trillion			1.2×10^{45}
Universe	2.0 trillion trillion trillion quadrillion			2.0×10^{63}

"Orders of Magnitude,"

Wikipedia, http://en.wikipedia.org/wiki/Orders_of_magnitude_(mass)

Figure 7: Evolution of the Universe and Life Timeline

	Millennium Ago	Generations (25 Yrs.)	Years Ago
The Big Bang	13,700,000		13,700,000,000
Nucleosynthesis	13,700,000		13,700,000,000
Star Formation	13,200,000		13,200,000,000
Milky Way Galaxy Formation	8,800,000		8,800,000,000
Solar System Formation	4,600,000		4,600,000,000
Simple Cells	3,600,000		3,600,000,000
Photosynthesis	3,000,000		3,000,000,000
Complex Cells	2,000,000		2,000,000,000
Sexual Reproduction	1,200,000		1,200,000,000
Multicellular Life	1,000,000		1,000,000,000
Fish	500,000		500,000,000
Land Plants	475,000		475,000,000
Insects	400,000		400,000,000
Amphibians	360,000		360,000,000
Reptiles	300,000		300,000,000
Mammals	200,000		200,000,000
Birds	150,000		150,000,000
Primates	75,000	3,000,000	75,000,000
Hominini	7,000	280,000	7,000,000
Homo Erectus	1,800	72,000	1,800,000
Homo Sapiens	200	8,000	200,000
Mitochondrial Eve	150	6,000	150,000
Y-Chromosomal Adam	140	5,600	140,000
Human Migration to South Asia	50	2,000	50,000
Human Migration to Europe & Australia	40	1,600	40,000
Domestication of the Wolf/Dog	15	600	15,000
Beginning of Agriculture	10	400	10,000
Beginning of the Calendar	2	80	2,000
Beginning of the United States	0	9	233

"Chronology of the Universe," Wikipedia, http://en.wikipedia.org/wiki/Chronology_of_the_universe
"Timeline of the Evolutionary History of Life,"
Wikipedia, http://en.wikipedia.org/wiki/Timeline_of_the_evolutionary_history_of_life
"Timeline of Human Evolution," Wikipedia, http://en.wikipedia.org/wiki/Timeline_of_human_evolution

CHAPTER 6

Evolution

What elegant simplicity! What an amazing story! Variation, competition, and the continuation of what works and the discontinuation of what doesn't work over and over again!

Like the first few seconds of the universe, the origin of the first cell and life is murky. The early Earth was frequently bombarded with asteroids and comets. Radioactive isotopes from supernova explosions were prevalent on early Earth.[55] It was a hot, radioactive, and violent place. Water from the comets most likely formed the oceans, and with a pH of roughly 5.5, it was quite acidic.[56] The atmosphere is thought to have been a mix of hydrogen, oxygen largely in the form of water vapor, carbon dioxide, hydrogen sulfide, and small amounts of nitrogen, carbon monoxide, and methane.[57]

Approximately 4.1 billion years ago, the Earth's crust cooled, the oceans formed, and conditions became right for organic compounds to self-assemble.[58] We know that when the conditions are right, the building blocks of life, namely amino acids, nucleobases, and phospholipids, as well as the RNA templates, naturally form. How these building blocks became DNA, proto cells, cell components, and the first cells is not yet fully resolved.

We do know that once basic cellular life started, evolution by natural selection gave rise to all the life forms that we know today. We infer this from two facts about populations: (1) more offspring are born than survive, and (2) heritable traits vary among individuals, resulting in differing rates of survival and reproduction.[59] The progeny of parents that survive and reproduce in the environment live on, increasing the frequency of the advantageous heritable traits in the population.[60] Mutation, sex, and recombination alter the traits and their expression in offspring.[61] The ever so slow generational, selective, and iterative process of natural selection creates the ever-changing diversity of life on Earth.

Mutations are changes in DNA sequences. They result from large sections of a chromosome duplicating and inserting into a gene, or small parts of several genes duplicating, recombining, and finding their way into a gene.[62] Ultraviolet radiation causes mutations. It was much more intense when life started three to four billion years ago than it is today.[63] Sex and recombination involve the unraveling of parent chromosomes and a mixed recombination of them. Sex and recombination do not alter trait frequencies within gene pools but do produce offspring with varying combinations of the parents' traits.

One of the first organisms, the chemoautotrophs, used carbon dioxide to oxidize inorganic materials approximately 3.5 billion years ago. A little later, prokaryotes evolved. Prokaryotes free energy from organic molecules such as glucose and store it as ATP, a process utilized in almost all organisms today. Photosynthesizing cyanobacteria evolved three billion years ago. They produce oxygen, and their arrival caused oxygen levels in the atmosphere to rise. Eukaryotic cells, membrane-bound organelles with diverse functions, appeared some 1.8 billion years ago.[64]

The evolution of life accelerated with the rise of sexual reproduction approximately 1.2 billion years ago. Sexual reproduction creates a far greater number of differences among offspring than mutations. The traits that aid survival are again "naturally selected" in the environment and over time become more prevalent in the population's gene pool.[65]

Protozoa emerged as little as one billion years ago. Later, some 580 million years ago, enough oxygen accumulated in the atmosphere to form the ozone layer, shield the Earth from much of the deadly ultraviolet radiation, and enable life to emerge on land. The earliest fungi evolved approximately 560 million years ago, the first vertebrates 485 million years ago, the first plants on land 475 million years ago, the first insects 400 million years ago, the first amphibians 360 million years ago, and the first reptiles 300 million years ago. The first dinosaurs appeared 225 million years ago, the first flowering plants 130 million years ago, and the first ants 80 million years ago. The earliest mammals arrived 200 million years ago, apelike animals 75 million years ago, Neanderthals 350 thousand years ago, and modern humans two hundred thousand years ago.[66]

Some 3.5 billion years have passed since life's beginning. To gain a sense of a billion years, consider that one hundred human generations span two thousand years, while fifty million human generations span a billion years. From the fossil records, carbon dating, and DNA records, scientists estimate that our species evolved from a more primitive one some 400,000 years, or twenty thousand generations ago.[67]

Today each of us is alive because of the successful struggle of some twenty thousand generations of human ancestors, as well as the successful struggles of all the species that preceded us. To think we are the result of 13.7 billion years of the universe's evolution and 3.6 billion years of proto cell, cell, organism, and species struggle is mind boggling and humbling. Just pondering the viruses, bacteria, insects, and natural predators that the twenty thousand generations of human ancestors overcame the last 400,000 years makes one realize the amount that some outcomes ripple through time. Consider that 400,000 years represents less than one-hundredth of a percent of the 3.5 billion–year period.

A study of the evolution of life reveals science's extensive understanding of most of the four billion–year sequence of events. The explanations are understandable. The evidence is varied, consistent, persuasive, and even overwhelming when one is not blinded by contrary belief and carefully considers it. DNA and cellular commonality provide much of the evidence. The anatomical and time-related progression of species, selective breeding changes, and the fossil record provide additional evidence. The experimental data from all branches of science on interim evolutionary processes and our understanding of how to manipulate life processes also add credence to the explanations.

Competition and Comparative Advantage

Competitions have determined which organisms, groups, and species have inhabited the Earth for some four billion years. They determine whose progeny and genes continue; whose perspectives, practices, and priorities continue; and which schools, universities, enterprises, governments, and countries continue.

Competition forces individuals and institutions to perform. It forces them to learn, prepare, work hard, and innovate. It winnows the slackers from the enterprising, the weak from the strong, the losers from the winners. It furthers the fitness and wellbeing of all the levels of human organization.

Only competition universally causes people to give their best efforts. Without competition, people conserve energy, take advantage of their positions, and freeload. Without competition, leaders and their constituents do less for one another.

When leaders and institutions dominate a people, region, or market, they do not perform as well as when their constituents and customers have alternatives. This is true for enterprises, schools, institutions, political parties, governments, religions, and countries. Alternatives create competition and encourage performance.

Though some participants in competitions lose, comparative advantage assures that there are opportunities for everyone. The comparative advantage insight originates in economics and explains the benefits of trade between countries.

> **Comparative Advantage** is the reality that when individuals or countries specialize and trade, each doing what he or she does relatively better, they all benefit. Even when one party does everything more efficiently than the other parties, all parties benefit from doing what they do best, selling some of their products and services, and using the proceeds to purchase what others do best.

Comparative advantage makes competition palatable. When we lose in one arena, if we keep trying, we succeed in other ones. If we do not make the high school basketball team, we may make the swim or volleyball teams; or if we are artistic, we might sing in the chorus, play in the band, or act in the drama club.

Even though some people might do all these activities better than us, they do not have time to do them all. If we search and persist, we find opportunities. Competition condemns no one to perpetual failure. Only resignation—something in our control—condemns us to perpetual failure. Because we do not have the time and strength to enter all competitions, and our opportunity to win some of them is greater than others, judicious selection of competitions improves our likelihood of success.

In most competitions, both the winners and losers benefit as the preparation strengthens the entrants. When we compete for a job and do not receive it, we practice and often improve our job application skills. When we compete for a position that requires training and certification, we benefit from the training and certification even if we do not receive the position.

Need stimulates our appetite for competition. Affluence diminishes it. Poorer people and populations rise, and affluent people and populations fall. When poor people do not have comfortable social safety nets, an hour of work improves their lives much more than it improves affluent people's lives.

As a population, we reap far more from competition than our individual winnings. Competition allocates positions and resources to those who most ably use them. It causes all the levels of human organization to function better. Our lives improve as each of these levels improves. When we award positions in a competitive manner and only retain those who perform well, the ablest people lead and work in our enterprises and institutions. The CEOs who competitively win their positions are the ones most likely to make their organizations thrive. The teachers who competitively win their positions usually are the best instructors. The police officers who competitively win their positions are the ones most able to keep our neighborhoods safe. Even if we do not participate in any of these competitions, we benefit from the better-functioning enterprises, schools, communities, and governments that result from the competitions.

Although few of us think about it, competition underpins our free enterprise system and representative democracy. We form our views of the world from the information we receive from competing news organizations. We select our products and services from arrays of competing ones. We choose our candidates for public office from numerous competing candidates, and our representatives select our policies, programs, and laws from a universe of competing ones.

This insight is important! It warrants wider circulation and greater appreciation. Competition improves the accuracy of our views. It lowers the cost and enhances the quality of goods and services. It improves the quality of our leaders and the effectiveness of our institutions, policies, programs, and laws.

A unionized workforce, one world government, and a world largely free of competition is a recipe for disaster. It is a recipe for subsistence, serfdom, and corruption. Living organisms pursue self, group, and others' interests in this order. This has been the case for billions of years, and it will not change in our lifetimes. Only competition transforms people's self-interest into community interest.

Without competition, leaders, political parties, journalists, and scientists do not have sufficient incentive to challenge one another's self-serving actions and inaction. They are less honest, do not work as hard, and do not innovate as much. History repeatedly demonstrates that the absence of competition invites mediocrity, stagnation, and corruption.

Without competition, those assigning jobs give them to their friends rather than to the best-suited applicants. Incompetent people become leaders, researchers, doctors, engineers, and teachers. Without competition, little works well, inefficiency increases, and living standards decline. While competition is hard on some individuals, it is necessary and its benefits far outweigh all other alternatives.

And despite what some people espouse, competition among countries need not perpetuate war. Countries can compete with one another and peacefully coexist when they (a) have access to needed resources, (b) stabilize their population growth, (c) maintain physical, technological, financial, and military fitness, and (d) have healthy relationships. We have only to look to the Swiss to see how this is done. In the middle of war-torn Europe, Switzerland has lived peacefully for more than 150 years; and they have done this by satisfying these four conditions.

> **Competition** is (a) two or more ideas, practices, or things contesting for some form of superiority, or (b) two or more organisms battling for territory, resources, mates, influence, and existence.

While the best leaders, teachers, coaches, and parents may choose to shield our youngest children from competition for four to five years, they otherwise embrace it. They understand that (a) competition creates individual, institutional, and population excellence, (b) competition is the most objective, fair, and effective method for allocating resources and positions, as well as for deciding which characteristics, individuals, enterprises, institutions, governments, and species advance, and (c) comparative advantage assures that everyone has opportunities.

Natural Selection and Gradualism

Before the 1800s, no one imagined that life was the handiwork of a simple natural process and billions of years. Natural selection, invisible and incomprehensible in one generation, becomes comprehensible over several generations. Charles Darwin, the first to recognize this process, wrote in 1859:

Owing to this struggle for life, any variation, however slight and from whatever cause proceeding, if it be in any degree profitable to an individual of any species, in its infinitely complex relations to other organic beings and to external nature, will tend to the preservation of that individual, and will generally be inherited by its offspring. The offspring, also, will thus have a better chance of surviving, for, of the many individuals of any species which are periodically born, but a small number can survive. I have called this principle, by which each slight variation, if useful, is preserved, by the term of Natural Selection, in order to mark its relation to man's power of selection . . . One general law, leading to the advancement of all organic beings, namely, multiply, vary, let the strongest live and the weakest die.[68]

Natural selection requires generations, inheritable traits, variation of the traits, and competition—conditions that are characteristic of all life. All organisms live, reproduce, and die. Their generations range from hours to hundreds of years, but in all cases, their lives follow this pattern. All organisms have offspring with a different mix of inheritable characteristics. Mutations, sex, gene recombination, and gene flow cause these traits to vary among organisms and across generations.

The offspring of all organisms inhabit competitive environments. If territory and resources initially are ample, organisms proliferate to the point that the territory and resources become in short supply. Thus, once life establishes in an area, territories and resources take work to acquire. The offspring that are better able to fulfill their needs and reproduce in an environment continue. They are "naturally selected" and increase the frequency of their traits in the population. This ever-so-slow, generational, and iterative process evolves all life forms.

Natural Selection is a natural process that requires inheritable traits, variation of the traits, generations, and competition, and

where those organisms better suited for their environments
place more offspring into the next generation, increasing the
frequency of the genes governing the advantageous traits.

As hard as it is to believe, bacteria, algae, fungi, worms, spiders,
bananas, frogs, crocodiles, robins, dogs, monkeys, and humans all result
from a long series of successive and infinitesimally small changes over
large spans of time. The concept of gradualism helps us understand evolution and the process of natural selection.

Gradualism is the reality that a series of imperceptible small
changes accumulate into tremendous, unrecognizable trans-
formations over large spans of time.

Consider the evolution of giraffes from a species similar in nature
to the zebra species. Some thirty to fifty million years ago, zebra-like
animals were numerous on the plains of Africa. Some of these zebra-like
animals had slightly longer necks and could graze the higher vegetation.
These animals could feed themselves, survive, and successfully reproduce when the vegetation closer to the ground became in short supply.
As these flourishing, longer-necked animals mated with one another,
more of their longer-neck genes populated this gene pool. As this process iteratively occurred over hundreds of years, a reach advantage of
inches became feet.

Giraffes with necks longer than modern giraffes did not do well.
Their necks were too long and interfered with daily life. These giraffes
did not fulfill their needs and reproduce. In this manner, natural selection lengthened the necks of giraffes to the point where longer necks
provided advantage in feeding, but not disadvantage in daily living.

The ability of the longer-necked animals to survive and successfully
reproduce provides an excellent example of how a series of small changes
accumulated into a pronounced one in the zebra-like to giraffe species
over numerous generations. Amazingly, each form of life has changed

and adapted to its environment in a similar manner, but because the process is glacially slow, it is mostly imperceptible to us.

The breeding of animals by humans for hundreds of years is an example of a directed selection process. We can see the handiwork of directed selection or "breeding" in dogs. From the Chihuahua to the Great Dane, all the breeds of dogs arose from a common gray wolf ancestor that lived some 130,000 years ago and people's selection of offspring exhibiting various traits over thousands of years.[69] World-renowned Harvard biologist E. O. Wilson writes:

> The theory of population genetics, and experiments on other organisms, show that substantial changes can occur in the span of less than 100 generations, which for man reaches back to the time of the Roman Empire.[70]

The domestic turkey, with which I have years of firsthand experience, is now over two hundred generations removed from the wild turkey. By selectively breeding the whiter-feathered, broad-breasted, fast-growing turkeys, breeders have created commercial breeds very different from the wild turkey in relatively few generations.

The evolution of life and natural selection become clearer to us as we learn to breed plants and animals. In fact, students can observe natural selection and evolution in shorter maturation species like fruit flies in college biology courses in just a few weeks.

Interrelated Products of the Past

> It is a mistake to think that the past is dead. Nothing that has ever happened is quite without influence at this moment. The present is merely the past rolled up and concentrated in this second of time. You, too, are your past; often your face is your autobiography; you are what you are because of what you have been; because of

your heredity stretching back into forgotten generations; because of every element of environment that has affected you, every man or woman that has met you, every book that you have read, every experience that you have had; all these are accumulated in your memory, your body, your character, your soul. So with a city, a country, and a race; it is its past, and cannot be understood without it.[71]

—Will and Ariel Durant

The universe is vast and repetitious, but it is also interrelated. It started from a point in time and space, expanding outward and continuing through time. The universe had a hot beginning and constantly changes as it cools. As it cooled, it coalesced into trillions of galaxies and trillions of trillions of stars, planets, and planetesimal bodies. Its living stars have assembled twenty-six of the elements, and some of its dying stars the remaining elements. The elements themselves have self-assembled into molecules, and some of the molecules into nucleotides.

Under the right conditions, it appears that nucleotides with the help of some vents deep in the sea assembled into RNA, DNA, numerous other amino acids, proteins, and one or more cells. The one or more cells started dividing and replicating itself or themselves. Under the direction of DNA and the selection pressure of an environment, some of the resulting cells formed multicellular organisms. Some multicellular organisms formed superorganisms. Just as the galaxies, stars, planets, planetesimal bodies, elements, and nucleotides occur throughout the universe, I believe we will one day learn that RNA, DNA, amino acids, proteins, cells, multicellular organisms, and superorganisms occur throughout the universe.

After the first cell or cells formed some 3.6 billion years ago, at least one of them became a reproductive dividing machine. This cell and its progeny outcompeted all other protocells. Since the formation of this cell and its progeny, no other cells seem to have formed from scratch. All the living cells that scientists have examined appear to come from divisions of this first dominant cell. One human body alone is comprised of several trillion cells. Imagine the cell divisions that have occurred from the original dominant cell throughout the last 3.5 billion years to form every bit of life and cell that has ever lived on Earth.

Germ cells, those in ovaries and testes and which start all forms of life, make the interrelatedness of life possible. They are immortal. They do not age. Under the right conditions and with access to the necessary resources, they may divide ad infinitum. It is the somatic cells, the rest of the cells that form our bodies, that age and die.

Thus, we share an interrelated past with all life on Earth. We share a common human ancestor with all other people and common ancestors with primates. We share common ancestors with mammals, reptiles, amphibians, insects, fish, and plants. And most amazing of all, we share basic nucleotide sequences of the first surviving cell with all terrestrial life forms.

Nature's Way

From the evolution of life, we discover a model for change that I call "Nature's Way." Nature's Way is an incredibly powerful approach that is advantageous to enterprises, institutions, and governments. The more we employ this approach in education, the more the students learn. The more we use it in businesses, the more our products and services improve. The more we apply the model to nonprofit organizations and government, the more their products and services improve.

> **Nature's Way** is the variation, competition, and the continuation of what works and discontinuation of what does not work over and over again.

The evolution of the universe and life is wondrous! Science reveals much about how the universe and life evolve but nothing about why they evolve. Implicit in the why is intent, and I see no more intent in evolution than in the flow of a river.

The universe and life as we know it are the cards nature deals us; and what matters is what we do with these cards—how we advantageously align with the flow; utilize our circumstances and gifts to advance our families, communities, country, and life; and bridge the 13.7 billion years past and the future.

Evolution—the gradual change of the universe, life, organization, government, culture, or something else over time. In the case of the evolution of life, it involves variation, inheritable traits, generations, comparative advantage, competition, and natural selection, where organisms better suited for their environments place more offspring into the next generation, increasing the frequency of the genes governing the most advantageous traits.

CHAPTER 7

Fitness

"To be or not to be?"

Shakespeare's character Hamlet, contemplating existence, poses the question of all questions. While some people ponder this question, most forms of life just want "to be" by nature. Underlying the actions of all forms of life and most every individual, family, group, institution, enterprise, country, and culture is an instinct "to be." If this were not the case, the organisms, individuals, groups, and organizations would "not be"; being is difficult.

Meritocracy

We have always needed territory, water, food, and shelter, and now, we need energy and many other resources. Our continuation depends on these things. For most of us, our ancestors secured our territory for us. Now, we only need to purchase or rent a small slice of it and contribute to its defense. We only need to be productive, earn our livelihoods, buy needed resources, and pay our taxes.

The defense of territory and procurement of resources for many in the West have become so easy that we forget that we require them. We forget that organisms and groups must win a long series of minor and major competitions for them. We forget that we only flourish as we prevent other life forms from taking our territory and resources. We hold our ground or we perish. This has been the reality for billions of years, and it will not change in our lifetimes.

As much as some of us would like to live apart from nature, remove ourselves from competition, and avoid the work of being fit, such thinking is fanciful and foolish. Individuals and institutions wither without competition and the winnowing of the fit from the unfit. One world order, a socialist state, monopolies, quotas, price controls, and socialism are futile pursuits. They are corrupting, debilitating, temporary, and contrary to evolution. Eventually, they give way to competitive and meritocratic arrangements.

> **Meritocracy** is the assigning of the fittest or the ablest and most qualified people to the available roles and positions within a group regardless of their age, gender, religion, race, or ethnicity.

In this chapter, I will only define meritocracy and note that it is an essential part of fitness. A more detailed discussion of it appears in a subsequent book, *Flourish: Winning Practices of Government and Enterprise*.

Procreation

Besides assigning roles and positions meritoriously, fitness requires procreation. It requires organisms to place as many or more offspring into the next generation as their competitors. Most forms of life are programmed to do this. It is in their DNA, and they cannot do otherwise. Humans have choice. Some choose to have fewer children and fewer domestic demands. Others decide to have several children. Those having fewer children often express concern about the finite human carrying capacity of the Earth. Those having several children play out the program that nature gives us.

Unfortunately, there is a downside to having fewer children that most people do not consider. Having fewer than 2.1 children per family on average steadily erodes the vitality of a population and culture. The population shrinks as other populations grow. Its ability to defend itself declines, and its culture, Winning Perspectives and Practices, and influence decline in the world.

> **Procreation** is the tendency for people to mate and parent children. Family sizes of 2.1 children per female maintain a population and larger ones increase it.

We may feel we would be happier without children, choose our career over having children, and think that having children strains the environment, but we need to replace and increase our numbers to maintain our relevance. We do not need to out-procreate every competitor, but we do need to maintain similar numbers through time. Our personal desires and concern for the Earth's ecology do not change our need for demographic and cultural fitness.

We may increase our population with immigrants, but immigrants who do not assimilate well and too many immigrants create minority subcultures and crippling division. They decrease the prevalence of a highly successful population's Winning Perspectives and Practices and their fitness. France, Germany, Greece, the United Kingdom, and Sweden currently have these problems.

So how do we maintain relevance, not overpopulate the world, enjoy a high quality of life, and not degrade the environment? In short, we work with other countries to reduce our and their population growth just as we work with them to reduce our and their nuclear weapons; and more specifically, we utilize the Winning Practices described in subsequent books.

Generally, we do not see the Islamic cultures as being particularly successful, but they are highly successful. Common to the Islamic cultures is Islam, the most Darwinian religion. Islam encourages its practitioners to have large families. We can see this by comparing the teachings of Islam with other religions and by examining the growth of Islamic populations over time.

Islamic populations have grown from 0 to 1.6 billion people, or 23 percent of the world's population, in just 1,400 years. No other group disperses, embeds, multiplies, and maintains their cultural identity within other cultures as well as Muslims.

Figure 8 compares the U.S., Islamic, and world populations over time. At current growth rates, Islamic populations will grow to 9.5 billion people and almost half of the world's population in one hundred years. Without immigrants, the U.S. population shrinks.[72] With immigrants, the U.S. population grows from 310 to 840 million people and decreases from 5 to 4 percent of the world's population.

Figure 8: Comparison of the U.S., Islamic, and World Populations Over Time

	2012 Population in Millions	Percent of Total Population	Percent Annual Growth Rate	Years to Double	Population After 100 Years in Millions	Percent of Total Population
U.S. Population	310	5	1.0	69	840	4
Islamic Population	1,600	23	1.8	38	9,530	46
World Population	7,000	100	1.1	63	20,900	100

"List of Countries by Population," Wikipedia
http://en.wikipedia.org/wiki/List_of_countries_by_population
"List of Countries by Muslim Population," Wikipedia
http://en.wikipedia.org/wiki/List_of_countries_by_Muslim_population
"List of Countries, by Population Growth Rate," Wikipedia
http://en.wikipedia.org/wiki/List_of_countries_by_population_growth_rate

Islam's unstated and underlying aim is population growth. It teaches its members to maintain their faith and distinctive dress, disperse throughout the world, have large families, and convert other people to their faith. It encourages its members to embed within populations, increase their numbers, and gradually change the ethnic mix, culture, and laws of a country. The real Islamic threat is not terrorism, but demographic and cultural in nature.

From an evolutionary perspective, Jewish populations have the meritocracy aspect of fitness right, and Islamic populations have the procreation aspect of it right. China steadily improves both, while most developed Western populations have both wrong.

Jewish populations emphasize merit a great deal. Islamic populations place less emphasis on it. China steadily becomes more meritocratic. The U.S. and European populations, which once heavily emphasized merit, emphasize it less now. The Jewish, American, and European populations shrink without immigrants.

Procreation and immigration are part of life, and what the Islamic populations are doing is nothing new and what life naturally does. They are just doing it more successfully now than other populations. In the seventeenth and eighteenth centuries, the English and Spanish populations were very Darwinian. They nearly annihilated the indigenous populations of North America, Latin America, South America, Australia, and New Zealand, and seeded these areas with their people and cultures. Their Darwinian actions during that time set up their dominance in the nineteenth century. Professor of geography at UCLA and Pulitzer Prize winner Jared Diamond indicates that such ruthless dominance has been the norm for thousands of years:

> Twelve thousand years ago, everybody on Earth was a hunter-gatherer; now almost all of us are farmers or else are fed by farmers. The spread of farming from those few sites of origin usually did not occur as a result of the hunter-gatherers elsewhere adopting farming; hunter-gatherers tend to be conservative . . . Instead, farming spread mainly through farmers outbreeding hunters, developing more potent technology, and then killing the hunters or driving them off of all lands suitable for agriculture.[73]

Those who think we have evolved beyond this Darwinian behavior are sadly mistaken. Such behavior has been the way of all life for millions of years. Our DNA carries instructions for ruthless domination, and whenever territory and resources are scarce, this behavior and self-righteous justifications for it emerge.

Thus, we can no more unilaterally decrease our procreative, political, economic, or military power as our nuclear power. Just as we only decrease our nuclear arsenal as our primary competitor, Russia, decreases its arsenal, so we must only decrease our procreation as China, India, Brazil, and the Islamic countries decrease their procreation.

A study of evolution, the universe, and life also suggests that one day we will face competition from extraterrestrial life. This is not certain but likely. The redundancy observed throughout the universe, the pre-disposition of the universe and life to self-assemble, and the existence of billions of potentially habitable planets suggest that the universe proba-bly is teeming with life. This insight raises a question that I often posed to my management teams over the years: Are we fit enough to withstand the competition from unknown as well as known sources?

The fitter organisms must have the offspring, and the offspring must realize as much of their potential as possible for a population to do well over time. Ironically, as Western countries grow more complex, those who are the least fit have many children and those who are most fit have few children.

Although our ancestors did not understand evolution, they worked out many advantageous practices to raise fit and well-adjusted children. The practices of postponing sex until marriage, marrying young, hav-ing larger families, and lifelong marriage gave us large numbers of well-adjusted, able children.

Contrast these past practices to the current practices of "hook-ing-up," separating, single parenting, and small family sizes, and one quickly gains a sense of our great procreative and child development failures. Where past generations focused more on the next generation, we focus more on ourselves. Birth control, abortion on demand, rec-reational sex, career-centric fathers and mothers, weak marriage com-mitments, sexually transmitted disease (STDs), and related infertility all diminish our population's long-term health, development, and viability.

Our culture's current practice of channeling one-third of its pub-lic resources to unfit and unproductive people is also counterpro-ductive. Such misplaced compassion increases poverty and human suffering over time. Channeling more of these resources into research and development, general fitness, and the colonization of space would enhance our fitness and benefit future generations more. In later books in this series, I discuss superior, less costly ways to empower people and reduce poverty.

To be clear, I am not suggesting that we should control procreation, but I am suggesting that our culture and policies should encourage fit people to have children and discourage unmarried and unfit people from having children. Although this approach might seem elitist and old-fashioned, it aligns with evolution and nature. Moreover, it diminishes human suffering and improves a people's health over time.

Consider the effects of the following six realities over time, first individually and then collectively. While each warrants concern, the collective warrants purposeful action. While each reality concerns us, the six realities together should terrify us, as they are tantamount to cultural suicide and the surrender of all we hold dear. They are a disaster for our great-grandchildren and should spur us to action.

1. At current growth rates, the number of Muslims in the world will increase by several billion in the next one hundred years.

2. Most Muslims have many perspectives and practices that are antithetical to traditional Western perspective and practices.

3. As the extremist members of these groups attack us, rather than decisively retaliate against the governments who fund them and the mullahs who instruct them, we only pursue those committing the violent acts. Rather than prohibit the entry of the zealous mullahs and Muslims into our country, we invite them and financially support many of them. Rather than acting to expeditiously end the conflicts and discourage future attacks, we act in a manner that prolongs the conflicts, maims our youth, and drains our treasury.

4. We have children at rates that do not sustain our population and culture.

5. Many of the people who have our children are the people least able to raise them.

6. Though our numbers decrease and Muslim numbers rapidly increase, we expend massive amounts of resources to advance democracy throughout the world.

We do not perceive or foresee many of the cumulative and long-term effects of our policies, programs, and practices. If we did, intelligent, caring, and compassionate people would change them, as so many of them diminish our lives and harm future generations.

The Underlying Aim of Life

Thomas Jefferson wrote in The Declaration of Independence:

> We hold these truths to be self-evident, that all [people] are created equal, that they are endowed by their creator with certain unalienable rights that among these are life, liberty, and the pursuit of happiness.[74]

Somehow, this declaration of people's equality before the law, and basic rights, now means to many people that life is primarily about the pursuit of happiness. This is so unfortunate, as those who pursue happiness seldom find it. In my experience, the happiest people are those who pursue fitness, or in other words, people who maintain their health, treat others well, apply themselves in school, make marriage work, parent children well, earn their livelihood, contribute to their communities, and mentor their grandchildren.

Happiness is not the aim of life. Fitness is the aim of life, and fitness is its own reward. Fitness brings us health, competence, and affiliation with other high-performing, winning people. It brings us the esteem of others, desirable mates, and long life. It brings us offspring and the continuation of our culture and institutions.

Evolution delineates our end and circumscribes our means. It gives us some latitude to be foolish in the short term but not in the long term.

It reveals that we cannot unilaterally curb our population growth or disarm, as such actions assure irrelevance and extinction.

We cannot pursue happiness and expect to be happy, but we can pursue fitness and find happiness in its pursuit. The sooner we make fitness our individual, familial, and collective goal, the sooner we will rediscover our way, enjoy greater success, and find greater happiness.

Fitness—the ability of organisms to flourish, procure needed resources, and reproduce relative to other organisms. Fitness is the underlying aim of life and its own reward.

CHAPTER 8

Human Nature

We avoid pain and pursue pleasure. We compete for resources, mates, and influence. We pursue our self-interest and children's interests first, our affiliated interests second, and others' interests third. These inclinations work on us twenty-four hours a day, seven days a week.

Scientists have persuasively demonstrated that genes direct the development of our bodies and our inclinations. Genes nudge us to engage in numerous behaviors that aid survival and perpetuate our DNA. If this were not the case, then we and our nature would gradually exit the evolutionary stage.

The consistent way our genes drive our inclinations results in common tendencies that we call human nature. Charles Darwin and Abraham Maslow did an excellent job characterizing human nature and identifying a hierarchy of human needs. My thoughts and many others in this area build on their insights.

Individual and Familial

Fundamental to all life is an inclination to seek pleasure and avoid pain. This is a life-preserving inclination. We eat food and drink water because they sustain us, alleviate pain, and bring pleasure. We procure clothing, shelter, and security because they protect us, comfort us, and alleviate pain. These tendencies are obvious and self-evident. We would not live long without them.

Other tendencies are psychological, less obvious, and often culturally shaped. We work to earn money to purchase the things that bring us pleasure and help us avoid pain. We work to obtain the esteem of others and for social acceptance. We tell the truth to gain our parents' approval and avoid their anger. In the last two examples, the pleasure sought and the pain avoided are not physical, but psychological. They are shaped by our genes, families, cultures, and environments.

We have strong inclinations to understand the world, develop, and actualize. We see these tendencies in our children. We devote large portions of our time and resources to learning and developing skills. We attend school for thirteen or more years and spend weeks, months, and years learning our jobs. We also want to play on the stage. If we have musical ability, we make beautiful music. If we have artistic talent, we create beautiful art. If we have athletic ability, we want to compete in athletic competitions. If we have leadership ability, we want to lead. We develop and deploy the predilections that others encourage.

We are self-centered creatures, especially when we are young. Life is about us. When we are parents, life is largely about our children and us. When we are grandparents, life is about our children, grandchildren, and us. We focus on ourselves and our progeny much more than on others. Self-centered tendencies diminish as we age, and they diminish much more if our parents, schools, workplaces, and culture teach us to care about others.

Because we evolved primarily at a time when there was more benefit to short-term thinking than long-term thinking, we are short-term oriented. We respond to short-term rewards more than long-term ones. Our short-term tendencies are most apparent in babies and young children. Infants and young children want what they want now. Without strong cultural conditioning to learn to defer gratification, these inclinations do not end with childhood. Adults who do not learn to defer gratification buy many things on credit rather than with cash. We want things immediately, even when waiting would bring us substantially more in the future.

Our short-term orientation comes not only from a natural impatience but also from a tendency to overweigh what is freshest in our minds. Recent memories dominate longer-term memories. For example, after a series of misfortunes, we become pessimistic. After a run of good fortune, we become overconfident. We want to invest in the assets that did well last year even though they cost more. We tend not to invest in the assets that declined in value last year even though they are more likely to appreciate in value.

Our short-term tendencies make many of the activities that lead to success in modern life difficult for us. They make studiousness, frugality, perseverance, and accomplishment difficult. They make rising after several defeats and exercising good judgment after several successes difficult.

Most of us also prefer small certain rewards to larger uncertain ones. This aversion to losses makes entrepreneurship and investing unappealing to most people, and it is a primary reason why entrepreneurs, investors, and others need substantial opportunities to profit. Without opportunities to profit, we are too risk-averse to start businesses, save and invest, and undertake many of the other activities that improve our lives.

We also have a strong desire to create homes and reside in aesthetically pleasing places. Homes are comfortable refuges, opportunities to actualize, and statements of social status. We spend many of our resources and much of our discretionary time procuring and shaping our homes.

Along with our individual nature, we have a strong familial nature. We want to love, be loved, procreate, and see our children and grandchildren flourish. If this were not the case, our species would not be doing well. Familial tendencies are so strong that they dominate adult motivation. These tendencies are reasonably self-evident. I discuss them in detail in a subsequent book, *Flourish: Winning Practices of Families and Education*.

Social

Along with our individual and familial natures, we have a social nature. At some point in our past, our ancestors found living in groups advantageous. In groups, they could better defend themselves. They could more easily build homes, grow food, kill five-ton mastodons, and clothe themselves. Edward Wilson observes:

> The only other mammalian carnivores that take outsized
> prey are lions, hyenas, wolves, and African wild dogs.

Each of these species has an exceptionally advanced social life, prominently featuring the pursuit of prey in coordinated packs . . . Primitive [humans] are ecological analogs of lions, wolves, and hyenas . . . And they resemble four-footed carnivores more than other primates by virtue of habitually slaughtering surplus prey, storing food, feeding solid food to their young, dividing labor, practicing cannibalism, and interacting aggressively with competing species. Bones and stone tools dug from ancient campsites in Africa, Europe, and Asia indicate that this way of life persisted for a million years or longer and was abandoned in most societies only during the last few thousands of years.[75]

Scientists consider organisms that ally with others to be superorganisms. Superorganism affiliation conveys fitness. It conveys strength of numbers, economies of scale, and opportunities to specialize, trade, and synergize.

A Superorganism is a subpopulation of a species bound together genetically, biologically, and sometimes culturally that functions and competes as a unit.

Ants form colonies, bees—hives, wolves—packs, lions—prides, gorillas—troops, and humans—families, clans, tribes, cities, states, and countries. Humans also form clubs, associations, enterprises, universities, international alliances, and countless others, and they belong to numerous superorganisms simultaneously.

Eons of natural selection have honed our social and superorganism nature, and thus, it serves our self-interest. We not only seek money to procure products and services that bring us pleasure and help us avoid pain, but we also seek it for the social status and influence it brings us.

We seek power and influence within the groups with which we affiliate to affect their agendas.

Surprising to most people but less so to students of evolution, altruism even serves our self-interest. Altruism is not just selfless concern for others. Rather, it is usually some self-interest wrapped in a concern for others. Altruism advances our standing within groups, increases our opportunities with them, and increases the likelihood of receiving aid from them. Journalist, scholar, and award-winning author Robert Wright writes in his landmark work, *The Moral Animal*:

> Altruism, compassion, empathy, love, conscience, the sense of justice—all these things, the things that hold society together, the things that allow our species to think so highly of itself, can now confidently be said to have a firm genetic basis. That's the good news. The bad news is that, although these things are in some ways blessings for humanity as a whole, they didn't evolve for the "good of the species" and aren't reliably employed to that end. Quite the contrary: it is now clearer than ever how (and precisely why) the moral sentiments are used with brutal flexibility, switched on and off in keeping with self-interest; and how naturally oblivious we often are to this switching. In the new view, human beings are a species splendid in their array of moral equipment, tragic in their propensity to misuse it, and pathetic in their constitutional ignorance of the misuse.[76]

Although the unselfish aspects of our nature ultimately serve our self-interest, we should not despair or become too cynical. Altruism, compassion, empathy, love, conscience, and a sense of justice are essential to group function. Affiliation only conveys fitness as people exhibit these characteristics, develop social cohesiveness, and work together. Altruism, compassion, empathy, love, conscience, and a sense of justice further

social cohesion and teamwork. Too much individualism and member separation erode the benefits of affiliation: strength of numbers, economies
of scale, and opportunities to specialize, trade, and synergize.

One final note on our social nature and tendency to affiliate is that
as we affiliate with others, we absorb their thinking and disregard information that challenges it. This human tendency furthers affiliation and
our opportunity to reap its benefits. It increases our ability to work with
others and strengthens the social cohesion of groups. And most of the
time, we are not even aware that we do this. Our tendency to absorb
others' thinking and disregard information that challenges it completely
eludes us when we are on the inside of a group. We only recognize it
when we are on the outside of a group looking in.

Once we understand our superorganism and social nature and its
importance, we realize that (a) the individual is not preeminent, (b) we
have individual, familial, and social natures, (c) we must balance the
requisites of these natures, and (d) sometimes individuals must sacrifice
themselves for the larger group.

Environmental Alignment

As long as we inhabit environments similar to the hunter-gatherer
environments from which we evolved, our genes do an excellent job of
driving our behaviors. This is because, as Edward Wilson notes:

> The selection pressures of hunter-gatherer existence have
> persisted for over 99 percent of human evolution.[77]

Different environments favor, or exert selection pressure on, different organism characteristics. The savannahs and forests of the hunter-
gatherer were no different. They favored relatively small, mobile groups,
or tribes, comprised of individuals who lived and worked together coop-
eratively to defend themselves and secure scarce nutrients.

When our environments become significantly different from the
hunter-gatherer environments and/or we confront foreign substances,

some of our genetic tendencies forged in the hunter-gatherer environment adversely affect us.

Environmental pressures take generations to shape our genetic inclinations. When our environment changes in just a few generations, as has been the case in the last 150 years, we must consciously direct our behaviors more and override some of our genetic inclinations. In rapidly changing environments, intelligence, leadership, enculturation, and discipline are critical to our success.

Tobacco, alcohol, drugs, caffeine, sweets, fats, salt, and pornography were not readily available throughout most of our evolutionary history. Natural selection has not had enough time to populate the gene pool with genomes that incline us to avoid these things. Thus, these pleasure-titillating substances and activities pose serious challenges to us. Once they pleasure our brains, we want more of them even though we know they can be addictive and harmful.

If we are fortunate, our parents, teachers, coaches, and mentors conditioned us to avoid many harmful behaviors and substances. If we were not so fortunate, we must develop an aversion to them or an ability to moderate our use of them.

Because it is tough for people to counter human nature on their own, we want to create laws, policies, institutions, and environments to mitigate these challenges for people as much as possible. Getting people to overcome the genetic inclinations that act upon them twenty-four hours a day, seven days a week is an uphill battle.

If we want to improve our families and institutions, we must utilize practices that are developed with a keen understanding of human nature. Ignorance of human nature fuels attempts to improve the world that have serious unintended consequences. David Brooks writes:

> I believe we inherit a great river of knowledge, a flow of patterns coming from many sources. The information that comes from deep in the evolutionary past we call genetics. The information passed along from hundreds of years

ago we call culture. The information passed along from decades ago we call family, and the information offered months ago we call education. But it is all information that flows through us. The brain is adapted to the river of knowledge and exists only as a creature in that river. Our thoughts are profoundly molded by this long historic flow, and none of us exists, self-made, in isolation from it.[78]

The genius of a prudently regulated free enterprise and market economy is that it works with human nature. It encourages people to pursue their self-interest in mutually beneficial ways and in ways that benefit the larger superorganism. The entrepreneurs who work hard to make a profit and their employees who work hard to earn additional pay improve the affordability and desirability of products and services. I discuss free enterprise and markets more in the subsequent book, *Flourish: Winning Practices of Government and Enterprise.*

Unlike free enterprise, socialism does not align with human nature. Groups of people who do not learn, work hard, raise able children, and evolve eventually find themselves at the mercy of the groups that do these things. People's rewards must vary with the risks that they take and their quality and quantity of work. People cannot be demeaned and ostracized for taking risks, working hard, and doing well, as they frequently are in socialistic arrangements.

Free enterprise offends our sense of fairness, but it improves our living standards because it works with human nature. Socialism appeals to our sense of fairness but diminishes our living standards because it does not work with human nature. I describe an arrangement that makes prudently regulated enterprise fairer in ways that avoid the unintended consequences of socialism in the subsequent book, *Flourish: Winning Practices of Government and Enterprise.*

Like socialism, labor unions run counter to harnessing the benefits of people pursuing their own self-interests. Like socialism, they appeal to our sense of justice, but they carry many negative unintended consequences. Unions are usually unfortunate responses to neglectful and/or abusive management, which do not replace the neglectful and/or abusive management and force counterproductive work rules on organizations.

Unions do engage management and temper its abusiveness, but they also divide the management and labor of organizations and create inefficiency. Unions force management to adopt work rules that reward seniority at the expense of merit and that incentivize people to coast, play it safe, and accomplish less.

Those who promote unions usually do so with the good-hearted intentions of raising middle-class wages and benefits. While unions do improve their members' wages and benefits in the short term, they make enterprises less competitive and often cause members to lose their jobs in the long term. They raise the prices of products and services and lower other people's living standards. Those who more critically consider the effects unions realize that members' gains are more than offset by consumer losses and the eventual loss of jobs, economic activity, and tax revenue.

Human nature is one of the cards nature deals us. It is not something that we can change in our lifetimes. Winning Practices and institutions harness human nature and stream positive effects. Losing practices and institutions ignore human nature and stream unintended negative effects. Understanding human nature and aligning our institutions, policies, and practices with it improve our fitness and wellbeing dramatically.

Human Nature—a collection of universal individual, familial, and social tendencies that help us to shape our institutions policies, and practices advantageously. It is the reality that we pursue our and our progenies' interests first, the interests of those with whom we affiliate second, and the interests of others last. We avoid pain and pursue pleasure; seek water, food, clothing, shelter, and security; and act to obtain others' respect and esteem, where the pleasure we seek and pain we avoid is physical and psychological. We desire to understand the world, develop, and actualize. We have a short-term orientation, an aversion to losses, and desire to live in aesthetically pleasing environments. We want to love, be loved, procreate. We want our children and grandchildren to flourish. We seek money, power, and influence, and we affiliate with others in mutually beneficial ways, absorbing much of their thinking, and disregarding information that challenges it.

CHAPTER 9

Periodic Disaster

Life is not without its challenges or for the faint of heart.
The universe and planet are violent and perilous places.

The Earth's fossil record indicates that more than half of all living species became extinct during five catastrophic periods, occurring approximately 200, 250, 370, 440, and 656 million years ago.[79] Mass extinctions do not happen very often, but they happen. When they do occur, they dramatically change the mix of species that inhabit the Earth.

Scientists do not know for sure the causes of these mass extinctions, but they hypothesize that supernova explosions, solar eruptions, asteroid impacts, planetary polarization changes, volcanic eruptions, and platonic shifts can alter climate and sea levels enough to cause them. These five catastrophic periods warn us that conditions can change drastically on Earth.

Along with dramatic climate changes, diseases and famines have devastated populations throughout history. Virulent viruses and bacteria reduced some European populations by more than 50 percent in the seventh, twelfth, and sixteenth centuries.[80] Famines accelerated the decline of the Egyptian, Roman, Mayan, and Byzantine empires.[81]

Historians estimate that famines reduced the populations of Central America (800–1000), France (1693–94), Iran (1870–71), Ireland (1845–49), Indonesia (1944–45), Cambodia (1975–79), and the Congo (1998–2004) by more than one million people. The former Soviet Union lost millions of people to famine during four periods in the last one hundred years: 1916–17, 1932–33, 1941–44, and 1947. China lost forty-five million people during the 1846–49 famine, sixty million people during the 1850–73 famine, another twenty-five million people during the 1907–11 famine, and millions more during the 1928–30, 1936, and 1959–61 famines. India lost millions of people during nine major famines that occurred between 1700 and 1950.[82]

War also has reduced populations throughout history. Figure 9 lists the major wars and conflicts with more than one-quarter of a million casualties. The figure shows that the world is never free of war. The figure should give people who maintain that we have evolved to the point where we no longer need a strong defense reason to reconsider this position.

The planetary record and history indicate that life must endure and overcome many hardships. They suggest that we would be wise to prepare for epidemics, famines, wars, and challenging times, to learn to deflect asteroids from hitting the Earth, and to develop technology to explore and to colonize space. Carl Sagan wrote:

> Since, in the long run, every planetary society will be endangered by impacts from space, every surviving civilization is obliged to become spacefaring—not because of exploratory or romantic zeal, but for the most practical reason imaginable: staying alive.[83]

We live in a rough neighborhood. The universe and Earth are dangerous places. It appears that no protective deity shields us from disasters. We are on our own. Our continuation depends on good fortune, numbers, preparation, fitness, and planetary and cosmic dispersion.

Periodic Disaster—*the reality that our universe and planet are dangerous places. Earthquakes, typhoons, tsunamis, tornados, wildfires, floods, famines, disease, and war regularly erode our populations. Quasars, supernovas, solar eruptions, asteroid impacts, planetary polarization changes, volcanic eruptions, and major platonic shifts periodically trigger significant climate and sea level changes that devastate or even eliminate many forms of life. Our continuation depends on fortune, numbers, preparation, fitness, the vitality of our planetary habitats, and cosmic dispersion.*

Figure 9: Major Wars and Conflicts
with Greater Than 250,000 Casualities

Kalinga War	262—61 BC
Second Punic War	218—201 BC
Gallic Wars	58—50 BC
Three Kingdoms War	184—280
An Lushan Rebellion	755—763
Muslim Conquests on the Indian Subcontinent	1100—1600
Mongol Conquests	1206—1324
Conquests of Tamerlane	1370—1405
Conquest of Mehmed II The Conqueror	1451—1481
Conquests of the Americas	1492—1691
French Wars of Religion	1562—1598
Japanese Invasions of Korea	1592—1598
Qing Dynasty Conquest of Ming Dynasty	1616—1662
Thirty Years' War	1618—1648
Wars of the Three Kingdoms	1639—1651
English Civil War	1642—1651
Third Northern War	1700—1721
War of the Spanish Succession	1701—1714
Seven Years' War	1756—1763
Napoleonic Wars	1803—1815
Shaka's Conquests	1816—1828
Taiping Rebellion	1850—1864
Crimean War	1853—1856
American Civil War	1861—1865

Dugan Revolt	1862—1877
War of the Triple Alliance	1864—1870
Mexican Revolution	1910—1920
World War I	1914—1918
Russian Civil War and Foreign Intervention	1917—1922
Chinese Civil War	1927—1949
Spanish Civil War	1936—1939
Second Sino-Japanese War	1937—1945
World War II	1939—1945
First Indochina War	1946—1954
Korean War	1950—1953
Algerian War of Independence	1954—1962
Vietnam War/Second Indochina War	1955—1975
Biafra War	1967—1970
Bangladesh Liberation War	1971
Ethiopian Civil War	1974—1991
Soviet War in Afghanistan	1979—1989
Iran-Iraq War/First Persian Gulf War	1980-1988
Somali Civil War	1986—Present
Civil War of Afghanistan	1989—1992
Second Burundian Civil War	1993—2005
War on Terror	2001—Present
Syrian Civil War	2007—Present

"List of Wars by Death Toll," Wikipedia
https://en.wikipedia.org/wiki/List_of_wars_by_death_toll

CHAPTER 10

Eco-Dependency

Our prowess and procreation serve us well until we outstrip the available resources or irrevocably harm our planetary ecosystems.

We and all of life have tremendous needs for natural habitats. Natural habitats do many things for us, and they do them at a lower cost and better than our best engineers. They provide fresh air to breathe, clean water to drink, and fertile soil to grow food.

Wetlands and floodplains filter water and reduce storm surges and flooding. Topsoil, earthworms, and bacteria provide us with a medium to grow food and a means to dispose of residue. Forests and grasslands filter water and convert carbon dioxide to oxygen. They provide timber, wood pulp, food, and animal feed. Mangroves, coral reefs, and oyster reefs filter water and protect coastlines. They and seagrass beds provide us with fish and seafood. Eco-dependency is the reality that we depend on natural habitats to provide us with clean air, clean water, fertile soil, food, and a hospitable climate.

Rachel Carson made many people aware of our negative impacts on our natural habitats and resources with her publication of *Silent Spring* in 1962. Since then, many scientists have systematically inventoried these impacts, and large portions of our population have learned about them. We now know that we have drained and developed millions of acres wetlands and floodplains. We have contaminated our ground-water, streams, rivers, and lakes with fertilizers, petroleum products, sewage, road salt, pesticides, herbicides, hormones, and other harmful substances. We have destroyed thousands of miles of mangroves, coral reefs, and oyster reefs and dumped millions of tons of trash into the seas.

We have cleared large forests and grasslands. We have significantly raised carbon dioxide levels in our atmosphere and contaminated it with carbon monoxide, nitrous oxide, sulfur dioxide, lead, and other particulates. We have scuttled ships with radioactive reactors and store approximately 74,000 tons of highly radioactive waste underground. The radioactive reactors and thousands of tons of radioactive waste must remain sealed and be safely stored for tens of thousands of years.[84]

Each year we destroy a few hundred of the estimated two million species that exist on Earth. Species destruction is irreversible and dangerous, as we and our habitats depend on so many species directly and indirectly. Species destruction negatively affects critical ecosystems, which in turn can negatively affect Earth's climate. All species have had a long and difficult past. E. O. Wilson writes:

> The worst thing that can happen during the [near term] is not energy depletion, economic collapse, limited nuclear war, or conquest by a totalitarian government. As terrible as these disasters would be for us, they can be repaired within a few generations. The one process ongoing in the [near term] that will take millions of years to correct is the loss of genetic and species diversity by the destruction of natural habitats. This is the folly that our descendants are least likely to forgive us.[85]

We cannot and should not attempt to preserve every species at all costs. Our resources are finite and the extinction of an unfit species is a natural part of evolution. However, it is in our interest to minimize our environmental footprint, protect as many species as practically possible, and identify and save the species that are critical to our ecosystems.

Asteroid impacts, polarization changes, volcanic eruptions, and other extraterrestrial shocks can dramatically change the Earth's climate, and now it seems that humans can as well. Scientists persuasively demonstrate that carbon dioxide (CO_2), methane (CH_4), nitrous oxide

(N_2O), and other greenhouse gases trap solar energy within the atmosphere and increase planetary temperatures. They estimate that postindustrial human activity adds some thirty billion metric tons of CO_2 to the atmosphere each year.[86] It is in our interests to find ways to reduce our greenhouse gas emissions.

Although the specific predictions of temperature, rainfall, and sea level changes associated with various human activities and the best ways to mitigate the negative impacts are controversial, most well-informed people agree that we are seriously harming the flora, fauna, and natural habitats on which we depend. They understand that we must mitigate our negative impacts as much as practically possible and slow the world's population growth.

Undoubtedly, enough of a change in the concentration of CO_2 and other greenhouse gases in the atmosphere will change Earth's temperatures and climate. Common sense alone suggests that photosynthesis (CO_2 depletion) must balance with respiration and fossil fuel use (CO_2 emission) over time for the climate to remain stable. Our deforestation of thousands of acres every year and tremendous emission of greenhouse gases should concern everyone. These activities are unsustainable and climate altering.

Deforestation and greenhouse gas emission represent externalities that governments should incentivize us to curb. What are externalities?

> **Externalities** are situations where one party's actions create a cost or a benefit to another party who did not choose to bear the cost or receive the benefit. Deforestation and CO_2 emissions are examples of externalities. The public, rather than the perpetrators, bears most of the cost of these activities in the form of sickness, disease, shortened lifespans, and climate change.

One of the best ways to address harmful externalities is for governments to tax them and incentivize individuals, institutions, and enterprises to reduce their emissions. If the government taxed CO_2 emissions, the emitters would raise the prices of their products to recoup the tax in the short term and develop more carbon neutral forms of energy in the long term. In response to the higher prices, the customers of large CO_2 emitters would reduce the use of their products, decreasing CO_2 emissions in the short term.

Taxing externalities is one of the best ways to reduce externalities because it does not specify how organizations and people must reduce them, but it does incentivize their reduction. It penalizes the undesirable activity and lets everyone use their ingenuity to find the best way to curtail the externalities.

Finally, we must protect our ecosystems all over the planet. We must clean up our act at home, and work with other countries to clean up their acts abroad. We may procure our oxygen, water, and nutrients locally, but ecosystems on the other side of the planet affect us. Heavy CO_2 emission in North America and Asia, deforestation in South America, and desertification in North Africa affect everyone.

Our lives and future depend on our ecosystems. Human activity is now sufficient to irreparably harm them. We must take common sense steps to reduce the harm. Carl Sagan writes:

> A tiny blue dot set in a sunbeam. Here it is. That's where we live. That's home. We humans are one species and this is our world. It is our responsibility to cherish it. Of all the worlds in our solar system, the only one so far as we know, graced by life.[87]

Eco-Dependency—the reality that we depend on many of the Earth's ecosystems, and we must minimize our impact on them as much as practically possible. We must use sustainable agricultural practices that protect groundwater and preserve topsoil, end the destruction of savannahs and forests, and help plants and trees repair damaged ecosystems.

Eco-Dependency involves developing environmentally friendly alternatives to harmful biological, chemical, and nuclear agents and responsibly disposing of the existing ones. It requires us to recycle our waste. It requires us to maintain historic carbon-dioxide-to-oxygen ratios and use carbon-neutral forms of energy. It requires us to work with other countries to reduce their adverse environmental impacts and curb the growth of the human population.

Winning Perspectives Summary

The Winning Perspectives indicate that we are perceptive, thinking beings who must both proactively and prudently look out for ourselves.

Truth, *like an accurate roadmap, enables us to grasp reality, trust one another, and work together.*

Causality *assures us that one or more causes underlie every event and that there exists a recipe for everything that happens.*

Scale *helps us understand the enormity of the universe and the minuteness of its building blocks. It reveals that each generation of life, while essential to life's continuation, lives for but a blink of an eye relative to all the generations of life. It provides us with a realistic view of the universe, its workings, and our place in it.*

Evolution, *the ultimate continuous improvement story, reveals the importance of competition and fitness. Comparative Advantage assures us that there exists an important role for each of us in life.*

Fitness, *or the ability of organisms to flourish, procure needed resources, and reproduce relative to other organisms, requires meritocracy and procreation. It brings us health, competence, and affiliation with high-performing, winning teams. It brings us the esteem of others, desirable mates, offspring, and lifelong wellbeing. It enables our families, institutions, communities, country, and culture to persist through time.*

Human Nature *is a collection of human tendencies that include (a) avoiding pain and seeking pleasure, (b) seeking others' approval, (c) loving others and being loved, (d) procreating, (e) being an individual, member of a family, and a member of various groups, (f) a short-term orientation, (g) risk aversion, and (h) the inclinations to pursue our self-interest and children's interests first, the interests of those with whom we affiliate second, and others' interests third. We cannot change human nature in our lifetimes. We are more effective and prosperous as we understand it, and align our lives, institutions, policies, and practices with it.*

Periodic Disaster *is the reality that our universe and planet are dangerous places and that our continuation depends on our ability to survive catastrophes, diseases, famines, and wars. It depends on some good fortune, numbers, preparation, fitness, the vitality of our planetary habitats, and cosmic dispersion.*

Eco-Dependency *is the reality that the Earth's ecosystems sustain us. It requires us to minimize our impact on the environment and to protect other species and the ecosystems as much as is practically possible. It compels us to maintain historic carbon-dioxide-to-oxygen ratios, use carbon-neutral forms of energy, and work with other countries to reduce their adverse environmental impacts and curb the growth of the human population.*

The Winning Perspectives provide direction. They help us distinguish Winning Practices and multiply our effectiveness. They have helped me immensely throughout my life. They have helped me determine how to live and be effective. I am confident they will do the same for you.

CHAPTER 11

Seven Levels
of Winning Practices

Because we find strength in numbers, economies of scale,
efficiencies in specialization, and synergy in working together,
we depend on multiple levels of human organization. We can do
everything right as individuals, but still have a miserable life if
our culture perpetuates dysfunction at the other levels.

Human life is complex. We live and act on many levels. We are born
into families, develop into individuals, and form families of our own. We
attend school, obtain work, affiliate with many groups, and reside in a
country. An individual, familial, and social tri-nature is embedded in our
genetic architecture and inclinations. It permeates and shapes our lives.

A lot must go right for us to become individually, familially, and collectively fit. We need a healthy set of genes, able parents, good schools,
profitable employment, functional governments, and helpful cultural
norms. As I thought about the practices that were necessary and sufficient for our fitness and well-being, I had the benefit of the Winning Perspectives, and I understood the practices needed to address seven levels
of human organization: government, enterprise, family, education, individual, group, and culture.

Government

The effects of governments, one of the most variable levels of
human organization, on their citizens range from extremely negative to
extremely positive. When government leaders are ignorant, incompetent, and misuse their powers, they harm their populations, sometimes
for generations. When they are wise, competent, and honorable, they
liberate and empower their populations.

Unfortunately, far more examples of poor governments exist throughout history than excellent ones. One just needs to study what life was like for people during the last four thousand years and to learn about life in Chad, Nigeria, Somalia, Sudan, Zimbabwe, Afghanistan, Syria, Yemen, North Korea, Laos, and Haiti to recognize this. Australia, Chile, Estonia, Hong Kong, Norway, New Zealand, Singapore, Switzerland, and Taiwan represent the few governments that do well by their citizens now.

Enterprise

Enterprises furnish us with a vast array of needed, desirable, and affordable products and services. Generally, they enable us to earn our livelihoods and support our families. They provide the means to pay for our schools, healthcare, and government.

Efficient, competitive, stakeholder-oriented, and growing enterprises are particularly important. They provide safer and more desirable work environments. They pay their employees well and provide better benefits and opportunities for advancement. They develop low-cost energy and eliminate many repetitive, menial jobs.

These enterprises give us the means to defend ourselves and enjoy secure neighborhoods. They enable one in four hundred people to provide our population with inexpensive, high-quality food products. They supply affordable, high-quality housing that allows many people to own their homes. They improve sanitary systems and deliver excellent healthcare. They provide us with computers, communication devices, and Internet access. They increase the number of products and services that we export, decreasing the relative cost of imports and enhancing the well-being of the country.

These enterprises create the wealth to fund government, make education universally accessible, and enable unprecedented amounts of free time. They fund research, continuously improve their productivity, and steadily raise our living standards. They generate the means for seniors to retire and for us to assist the people unable to provide for themselves.

Family

Our parents shape us before we shape ourselves. They each pass half of their genes to us and teach us innumerable perspectives and practices. Usually, they, more than anyone else, influence who we become and what we do.

Human maturation is a tremendous amount of work and takes years. It requires love, discipline, perspective, instruction, resources, and opportunities. It requires lifelong role models and mentors. It compels us to learn to modulate our emotions, defer gratification, and persevere. It requires us to learn the Practices of Individual and Group Effectiveness, which I discuss in the fourth book of the series, *Flourish: Winning Practices of Individuals and Groups.*

Human maturation requires able and engaged mothers, fathers, and grandparents. The human life span is three rather than one generation because parents and grandparents improve the survival and reproduction rates of their progeny. They do for children what no other level of human organization does for them. Children lacking functional families struggle much more than those who have the benefit of them.

Education

Education enables us to acquire the knowledge and skills that we need to provide for ourselves and successfully raise a family. We are born with instincts to guide us, but education supplements these instincts. It gives us access to the immense reservoir of perspectives and knowledge accumulated by others over time.

Effective schools provide children with the opportunity to learn to play, interact, and work with others. They provide children with able role models and mentors. They help children to form enabling habits and avoid debilitating ones. They teach children basic reading, writing, speaking, and math skills. They teach them the scientific method and science's findings regarding the evolution of the universe, Earth, and life. They convey to children our multicultural heritage, provide them with a sense of history, familiarize them with our knowledge base, and teach them specific career skills. They teach children the Winning Practices of Individual and Group Effectiveness.

Effective schools teach children about the real world and what works best. They provide children with a smorgasbord of activities to discover and develop their aptitudes. They expose children to different types of art and music and teach children to speak foreign languages, to be physically fit, and to win and lose. They provide children instruction about good government, free enterprise, and free markets. Effective schools teach children to be frugal and to invest their money wisely.

Education is more important today than ever before, as life is so complex. As science, technology, computers, and the Internet develop, the complexity of our work, products, and life increases. Today's foods, fabrics, materials, homes, appliances, cars, phones, and medical services are so much more specialized and technical than those of just one hundred years ago.

Individual

This level is particularly important as we are first and foremost individuals. Our genes incline us to pursue our individual and familial interests first, the interests of those with whom we affiliate second, and others' interests third. The effectiveness of the other levels depends on the competencies of the individuals that constitute them.

Millions of years of natural selection have hardwired these tendencies into us, and they act unconsciously on us twenty-four hours a day, seven days a week. We must consider this in all the other levels of human organization. Failure to recognize and harness human self-interest is a primary cause of unintended consequences and organization ineffectiveness.

Group

Although we do not form functional groups as readily today as we did decades ago, we still are members of numerous groups. Our groups may be educational, professional, political, social, recreational, or religious in nature.

In groups, we learn, earn our livelihoods, further common objectives, provide and receive services, socialize, and play. Often taken for granted, groups and organizations enhance our fitness and well-being. They provide us with protection and opportunities to socialize and learn from others. They allow us to specialize, realize economies of scale, and synergize. They offer us opportunities to develop leadership and team skills. They enable us to aid those who lack resources.

Culture

Culture orchestrates group activity. It assists us with the universal challenges of leadership, defense, the ownership and use of property, and the procurement and division of resources. Culture helps us with our roles as children, students, spouses, employees, parents, grandparents, and citizens. It helps us with discipline, conflict resolution, spouse selection, and aging. It assists us with the admittance of people into groups, the assessment of people's standing within them, and the removal of people from the groups.[88]

Culture works because our genes incline us to belong to groups and seek the esteem of others. Our genes incline us to avoid the pain of loneliness, disapproval, and ridicule. They cause us to feel pride when we please others and shame when we disappoint them. We want to be "good" as opposed to "bad" members of groups, where good involves loyalty and service to the group, and bad involves disloyalty or harm to the group.[89]

We naturally are comfortable with those like us and uncomfortable with those unlike us. Affiliation divides people into a "we" and a "they," and our nature causes us to treat those within our groups more favorably than those outside our groups. In fact, we have within us the ability to demonize, plunder, kill, and wage war against members of other groups.

> **Culture** is the perspectives, practices, and taboos that parents, teachers, and others transmit to us, and the art, heroes, and achievements that groups celebrate to reinforce the transmission.

Culture is human software that orchestrates our activity and is one of the most powerful forces on the planet. Families, schools, and religions teach our perspectives and practices to us. They pass their beliefs to us. We modify our practices, particularly those affected by technology, more easily than our perspectives and beliefs.

Heroes play a major role in sustaining and transmitting culture. The people we celebrate and shun signal the acceptableness of various behaviors and activities. Heroes consist of mythical figures and our parents, siblings, and teachers for most of us early in our lives. Later, they may be famous leaders, athletes, musicians, and actors.

Common cultural norms form around history, relatedness, gender, age, physical appearance, dialect, education, profession, living standard, political affiliation, ethnicity, language, and religion. What groups deem acceptable and unacceptable, or laudable and shameful circumscribes our behavior. Their norms affect what we do, what we do not do, and what we become over time. Every culture is the total of an incredibly large number of individual actions.

Countries' cultures and social cohesiveness matter. Countries constitute our largest groups. They are modern day tribes. A study of large groups, tribes, and countries reveals cyclical patterns of division and merger. Divisions occur when groups split in two, and mergers occur when groups unite. Because we lived in tribes for most of human history, divisions typically took place when two leaders, each with the support of a viable portion of a tribe, went their separate ways. Mergers, on the other hand, occurred as the men of one tribe killed the men of another and absorbed the women. In both cases, leaders drove the divisions and mergers. Variation in leadership strength and tribal cohesiveness precipitated the divisions and the mergers.

Today, corporations exhibit slightly more civil forms of divisions and mergers. Their divisions and mergers adhere to a legal process. However, this is not the case with countries. Their divisions and mergers, although rare, are civil and violent. When collections of disparate people aggregate into a country, and its leaders misuse their power, the country may break up, as happened to the former Soviet Union and some of the Eastern European countries. These were relatively civil separations. The recent breakup of the Ukraine provides an example of a violent separation. Sometimes, divided peoples merge. This was the case with East and West Germany and might be the case one day with North and South Korea.

Sociologists have found the decay of culture and decline of social cohesiveness in conjunction with the rise of a periphery culture to be the primary cause of the disintegration of many groups.[90] Cultural vitality and social cohesion play an immense role in the long-term success of a people. Charles Darwin wrote in *The Descent of Man*, 1871:

> A tribe including many members who, from possessing in
> a high degree the spirit of patriotism, fidelity, obedience,
> courage, and sympathy, were always ready to aid another,
> and to sacrifice themselves for the common good, would
> be victorious over most other tribes.[91]

Culture is the level of human organization most taken for granted and least understood. Like the air we breathe, it is essential but remains unnoticed until it fails. Culture affects our interpretations of the world, attitudes, choices, and actions. It affects our ability to be led, work in teams, and win. It affects the effectiveness of all the other levels of human organization.

The Seven Levels of Human Organization are government, enterprise, family, education, individual, group, and culture. The fitness and wellbeing of a people vary directly with their employment of Winning Practices at each of these seven levels.

We need each of these Seven Levels of Human Organization to thrive. Every one of them matters. They not only affect us, but also affect our children, grandchildren, and beyond.

The Path of Fitness

Some cultures steadily improve the lives of increasing numbers of a population better than other ones. This steady improvement of a people I call "The Path of Fitness."

> **The Path of Fitness** is the collection of perspectives and practices that cause a people to flourish by steadily increasing the portion of the population that have (a) a healthy diet and clean water, (b) adequate clothing and other necessities, (c) basic marital and family rights, (d) quality healthcare, (e) desirable choices regarding residency, education, and occupation, (f) safe and advantageous employment, (g) sustainable lifestyles, and (h) three-generation life expectancies.

Before the 1960s, the U.S. culture, for the most part, moved us along on the Path of Fitness. It steadily increased the proportion of people who enjoyed the benefits listed above. Not everything was perfect. Women and minorities needed to be included more, and we needed to live more sustainably. We needed to correct these shortcomings but otherwise were on the Path of Fitness.

Cultural Relativism

Introduced in an earlier chapter, Cultural Relativism, a concept found in anthropology and sociology and widely accepted in most academic institutions, is a worldview that has slowed our forward motion.

> **Cultural Relativism** is the idea that no culture is inherently better than another, and no one has a basis to judge the perspectives and practices of people of other cultures.

The fact is that some cultures convey fitness and well-being to their people, move them along the Path of Fitness, and persist through time better than other ones. In this sense, some cultures are better than others.

While cultural relativism furthers intercultural harmony and makes people feel good, it suspends critical judgements! For example, the cultures of Haiti and Singapore or North Korea and Switzerland clearly are not equally desirable. Viewing all cultures as equally desirable is like viewing all student work as equally meritorious. Not making distinctions between sloppy and well-organized work, factually correct and incorrect work, and dysfunctional and functional negatively affects learning. To be effective, successful, and persist in life, we must make qualitative distinctions and teach our children to make them. We must distinguish between winning and losing perspectives and practices.

So how do we further cultural harmony and differentiate between winning and losing perspectives and practices? We let others—who mean us no harm and do not infringe on our freedoms and rights—be. Then we critically examine their perspectives and practices, reject and stigmatize those that yield poor results, and adopt those that yield superior results.

Half a century after the cultural relativism nonsense started, a much smaller proportion of our population understands and acquires a full complement of Winning Perspectives and Practices. Many more people struggle. Our living standards, accomplishments, influence, and country decline.

Winning Practices

If we study the sciences, we learn that scientists have formulated few laws and that they do not view any of the laws as absolutes. The universe is immense, life is complex, and both are redundant.

The few causal relationships that scientists have determined only qualify as laws as substantial empirical evidence supports them, no contradictory evidence disputes them, and the relationships hold throughout the universe. When new observations contradict an established law, scientists reformulate the law.

Similarly, upon gathering the collection of Winning Practices for this book, I realized that few practices qualify as a Winning Practice, and that we should not view the chosen ones as absolutes. Human life comprises innumerable dynamic interrelationships, and once we move from the physical to the human realm, the causal relationships are less clear. They are seldom obvious, instantaneous, simple, and replicable.

Viewing a practice as a convention or one of many possibilities is superior to seeing it as "the right way" to do something. This may not be apparent when we are young and have not traveled much, but it becomes apparent as we gain experience. There are so many ways to do something. Our approaches are merely a subset of a larger set of possibilities. They may or may not be the best ones. Thus, it is better to think of our practices as best for the time being and not best for all of time.

> **Best Practice** is the approach out of all the known possible approaches that yields the most desirable effects.

The concept of a best practice is a superior way to view our practices because it conveys temporariness and openness to change, which in turn facilitates adaptation, improvement, and fitness. Just as avoiding certitude in science promotes the development of more accurate theories and laws, so does avoiding certitude in our daily lives. A practice or best practice is supreme only until we find a better one.

Although the concept of a best practice is helpful, eventually I found a serious problem with it: People evaluate the desirability of practices differently. Most people only care about a best practice's short-term effects on themselves or their group. Few people care about a practice's long-term effects on themselves, others, and our ecosystems.

For example, it may be a best practice for some people to refuse to work overtime. They may have all the money they need, so taking time off to perform household duties and parent children are better uses of their time. However, from the standpoint of their employers and colleagues, their decision to refuse overtime is not a best practice. Rather, the best practice when the interests of employers, colleagues, and family members are all considered may be to inform the employers that they do not want to work overtime, but they would work some overtime when it is critical to the business.

We may consider buying a new car, taking good care of it, and keeping it for several years to be a best practice. We may see it as a best practice because it eliminates the risk of acquiring an unreliable form of transportation associated with purchasing used cars, and it costs less than selling our car and buying a new one every two to three years. However, this practice may not be a best practice when we have limited credit and need to borrow money to purchase the car. The additional financing costs and debt may more negatively affect our lives than an occasional problem with owning a quality used car.

To counter these limitations, I developed the concept of Winning Practices. Winning Practices take more time to identify and develop but generate far fewer negative effects. They consider a practice's effects in five ways: (1) on the individual, (2) on the group, (3) on the environment, (4) in the short term, and (5) in the long term.

> **Winning Practices** are actions that positively affect individuals, groups, and/or the environment in the short and long term.

We align our lives with Winning Practices or we forgo their positive effects. We convey Winning Practices to our citizens or we forgo the benefits that they bring to our families, institutions, enterprises, and governments. We curtail losing practices or we reap their ill effects.

CHAPTER 12

Toward Truth, Freedom, Fitness, and Decency

If we make up our minds that this is a drab and purposeless universe, it will be that, and nothing else. On the other hand, if we believe that the Earth is ours, and that the sun and moon hang in the sky for our delight, there will be joy upon the hills and gladness in the fields, because the Artist in our souls glorifies creation. Surely, it gives dignity to life to believe we are born into this world for noble ends, and that we have a higher destiny than can be accomplished within the narrow limits of this physical life.[92]

—Helen Keller

Our lives depend on a habitable planet, territory, resources, a larger community, a home, a workplace, a healthy set of genes, parents, children, grandchildren, other family members, and friends. Beyond these things, our lives depend on Winning Perspectives and Practices.

Winning Perspectives describe our context. They suggest our means and end, as well as a need for an aspirational philosophy of life aligned with reality, nature, and human nature. Winning Perspectives help us identify Winning Practices.

The Winning Perspectives and our history suggest that Truth, Freedom, Fitness, and Decency are four of the most crucial Winning Perspectives and Practices, where:

> **Truth** is accurate approximations of reality, natural processes, and depictions of current and past events.

Freedom is the ability to fulfill our needs, think, speak, associate, travel, work, marry, have children as we choose, author our lives, and actualize.

Fitness is the ability of organisms to flourish, procure resources, and reproduce relative to other organisms.

Decency is treating others who mean us no harm with respect and consideration and as we want them to treat us.

Truth enables us to understand our context. Freedom allows us to author our lives. Our freedoms end where others' freedoms start. Fitness is the underlying aim of life. Decency endears us to others, enables us to work with others, and furthers specialization, trade, win-wins, and synergy. Together, Truth, Freedom, Fitness, and Decency enable us to multiply our strength and our prodigy and to persist through time.

Our most powerful understanding of truth comes from science. Our sense of freedom comes from living in our country. Our understanding of fitness comes from evolution, and our sense of decency comes from our Judeo-Christian heritage.

Fitness is our end. Truth, Freedom, and Decency are our noble means. Devotion to them gives our lives meaning. They further our effectiveness and wellbeing. They help us bridge the cultural divide.

The Winning Practices describe in more detail how we flourish within our context. They address the Seven Levels of Human Organization and comprise an unusually practical philosophy of life that aligns with reality, nature, and human nature.

Helen Keller was the first blind, deaf, and mute person to earn a bachelor of arts. She was also an accomplished author, political activist, and lecturer. It's hard for us to imagine her early life and all that she overcame. It is also equally hard for us to comprehend the difference that her life has made in the lives of all subsequent handicapped people.

It would have been easy for Helen Keller to find life meaningless, but her parents and blind teacher, Ann Sullivan, had other ideas. They sought to free Hellen Keller from her blindness, deafness, and muteness. And so it is with us: although we find no intent in nature, as perceptive, thinking, able, imaginative social beings, we may fill our lives with intent and meaning "beyond the narrow limits of this physical life." The Winning Perspectives and Practices help us do this. They not only describe our context and how we may flourish in it, but they reveal what matters and help us actualize and persist!

Figure 10 lists in italics the eight Winning Perspectives discussed in this book and the thirty-six overarching Winning Practices that I discuss in the next three books of the series:

Winning Practices of Government and Enterprise

Winning Practices of Families and Education

Winning Practices of Individuals and Groups

An abreviated version of books I-IV, as well as an innovative way to increase their prevalence in our population, may be found in the fifth book of the series:

Winning Practices of a Free, Fit, and Prosperous People.

Figure 10: The Flourish *Series*

Book I: Toward Truth, Freedom, Fitness, and Decency

Losing Our Way

Winning Perspectives
Truth
Causality
Scale
Evolution
Fitness
Human Nature
Periodic Disaster
Eco-Dependency

Seven Levels of Winning Practices
Toward Truth, Freedom, Fitness, and Decency

Book II: Winning Practices of Government and Enterprise

Winning Perspectives
Seven Levels of Winning Practices
Problems with Democracies

Government of the People
Powers, Prohibitions, and Structure
Freedoms, Rights, and Responsibilities
The Rule of Law
Inclusion and Meritocracy
Prudent Taxation
Financial Strength
Savings Accounts and Social Safety Nets
Consumer-Driven Healthcare
Assimilation
Peace through Strength
Sustainability

Free Enterprise and Markets
Responsible Corporate Governance
Prudent Regulation
Enterprise Competitiveness

Winning Culture

Book III: Winning Practices of Families and Education

Winning Perspectives
Seven Levels of Winning Practices

Spouse Selection
Marriage
Responsible Parenting
Empowering Habit Formation

Research and Knowledge
Education and Life Preparation
Parental Choice
Results-Oriented Education

Winning Culture

Book IV: Winning Practices of Individuals and Groups

Winning Perspectives
Seven Levels of Winning Practices

Health and Renewal
Thought
Priorities and Integrity
Proactivity
Excellence
Thrift and Investment

Affiliation
Decency and Caring
Understanding
Leadership
Teamwork
Improvement

Winning Culture

Book V: Winning Practices of a Free, Fit and Prosperous People

A shorter version of Books I-IV in one volume.

Acknowledgments

It is impossible to name all the people who directly and indirectly influenced my thinking. Included are some of the greatest leaders, thinkers, explorers, and innovators in history. Their thoughts and work enable us to realize the best of what life offers. The endnotes and Appendix A sections provide the names of many of these people.

Though many people have provided feedback to me concerning the content of this manuscript, their mention here does not mean that they endorse the perspectives and practices in it. I am solely responsible for its content.

In the preparation of this book, I thank my beautiful and ever supportive wife, Leokadia, my sons, Karl and Asher, daughters-in-law, Kristi and Kalee, and my extraordinary mother and father. I would like to thank my faithful and talented administrative assistant, Sherri Woods; insightful and encouraging editor, Deborah Grandinetti; patient and wise publicity counsel, Jane Wesman; energetic and able social media publicist, Autumn Glading; longtime graphic artist, Patty Schuster, photographer, Michelle Reed; and the brave and thoughtful members of my advisory board, Susannah Adelson, Roxanne Parmele, Barb Quijano, and Russ Smith. I also want to thank Justin Branch, Rachael Brandenburg, Karen Cakebread, Steven Elizalde, Jen Glynn, Tanya Hall, Jay Hodges, Carrie Jones, AprilJo Murphy, Pam Nordberg, Chelsea Richards of Greenleaf Book Group.

I thank Rolly Anderson, Bill Burrows, Jon Carroll, Jim Cohen, Mark Danni, Katherine Davies, Paul de Lima, John Doyle, Evan Dreyfuss, Brian Dunsirn, Bill Ellis, Tom Embrescia, Tom Ewert, Gary Fenchuk, Dan Fisher, Had Fuller, Dick Glowacki, Clint Greenleaf, Suzanne Heiligman, Jim Howe, Richard Kaufman, Deborah Keller, Michael Korchmar, Jim Jameson, Ken and Amy Lockhard, Steve McConnell, Steve McMahon, Jean Merrell, Carole-Ann Miller, Bill Morton, Dr. Story Musgrave, Mark Nielsen, Rosemary Perez, Jack Reinelt, Ed Schifman, Lindsay Schlauch, Mitch Sill, Haisook Somers, Ed Telling, Bob Vanourek, Jennifer Lehmann Weng, and Carl Youngman for their input and/or encouragement.

I thank Bella Stahl and the exceptional team members of CNY Feeds, the dedicated staffs of the Syracuse YMCA, Northwest YMCA, and Florida Nature Conservancy, and the incredible staffs and members of the International YPO-WPO and CEO organizations. I am also appreciative of all the people who spent hours developing Google, Wikipedia, and Wikiquote. Their efforts made finding and recalling information so much easier and enriched the content of this book immeasurably.

Additional Presidential Constitutional Failings

GEORGE H.W. BUSH

Gramm-Rudman Act of 1985

Americans with Disabilities Act of 1990

Military Action in Kuwait without a Declaration of War

BILL CLINTON

Medical and Family Leave Act of 1993

The Brady Handgun Violence Prevention Act of 1993

The Violent Crime Control and Law Enforcement Act of 1994

Use of the Line Item Veto, Which Is Unconstitutional

Deployment of the U.S. Military 41 Times around the World

Sodomization of a White House Intern and Untruthful Testimony

Additional Supreme Court Constitutional Failings

Home Building & Loan Association v. Blaisdell (1934) enabled governments to interfere with contracts between private parties.[93]

Helvering v. Davis (1937) gave Congress the green light to redistribute wealth. It gave Congress a free hand to legislate without judicial review.[94]

United States v. Carolene Products (1938) enabled federal and state governments to pass legislation that significantly devalues property without compensating the owners. It enabled the government to infringe upon citizen and enterprise economic liberties without judicial review.[95]

Wichard v. Filburn (1942) extended the federal regulatory authority to nearly every economic activity. It enabled the federal government to regulate economic activities that were not interstate and not commerce. It ended the principle that the federal government only has the powers expressly granted to it in the Constitution.[96]

Chevron U.S.A. v. Nation Resources Defense Council (1984) gave the departments and agencies of the Executive Branch the power to interpret the law.[97]

Bennis v. Michigan (1996) gave the government the authority to seize the property of innocent people without judicial hearings.[98]

Whitman v. American Trucking Associations (2001) enabled Congress to pass poorly defined laws and let unelected regulatory agencies fill in the details.[99]

Gutter v. Bollinger (2005) gave institutions the right to use racial preferences in their admittance procedures.[100]

Kelo v. City of New London (2005) gave governments the right to use eminent domain to take private property for economic development.[101]

Special Sources

Giants

The Ten Commandments	Moses
The Art of War	Sun Tzu
The Apology of Socrates	Plato
The New Oxford Annotated Bible with the Apocrypha	
Ninety-Five Theses, Catechisms, Lecture on the Papacy, and On Temporal Authority	Martin Luther
The Principia[a]	Isaac Newton
The Declaration of Independence	Thomas Jefferson
An Inquiry into the Nature and Causes of the Wealth of Nations	Adam Smith
The Pennsylvania Constitution of 1776	Benjamin Franklin et al
The Constitution of the United States of America and the Bill of Rights	Hamilton, Madison, Morris, Washington et al
The Federalist Papers	Hamilton, Jay, Madison
On the Origin of Species	Charles Darwin
General Relativity; Special Relativity[b]	Albert Einstein
I Have a Dream	Martin Luther King, Jr.
Lee Kuan Yew: The Grand Master's Insights on China, The United States, and the World[c]	Lee Kuan Yew

Significant

Berkshire Hathaway Annual Reports	Warren Buffett
The 7 Habits of Highly Effective People	Stephen Covey
Life Evolving	Christian de Duve
A Universe of Consciousness	Gerald Edelman
Capitalism and Freedom; Free to Choose	Milton Friedman
Jews, Confucians, and Protestants	Lawrence Harrison
Cosmos; Dragons of Eden; The Demon-Haunted World	Carl Sagan
Winning[d]	Jack Welch
Ants; On Human Nature; Consilience; The Future of Life	E. O. Wilson

Very Helpful

As a Man Thinketh	James Allen
Big History	Benjamin, Brown, Christian
The Little Book of Common Sense Investing	John Bogle
The One Minute Manager	Blanchard, Johnson
How to Win Friends and Influence People	Dale Carnegie
The Richest Man in Babylon	George Clason
Good to Great	Jim Collins
Aerobics	Kenneth Cooper
Jews, God, and History	Max Dimont
Leadership Is an Art	Max DePree
The Power of Habit	Charles Duhigg
Civilization: The West and the Rest	Niall Ferguson
Common Sense Economics	Gwartney, Lee, Stroup
Sapiens: A Brief History of Humankind	Yuval Noah Harari
Dune; Dune Messiah; Children of Dune	Frank Herbert
How the Scots Invented the Modern World	Arthur Herman
Culture and Organizations	Hofstede, Hofstede, Minkov
Men Are from Mars, Women Are from Venus	John Gray
The Story of the Earth	Robert Hazen
Life Ascending	Nick Lane
9 Presidents Who Screwed Up America	Brion McClanahan
The Dirty Dozen	Levey and Mellor
The Road Less Traveled	M. Scott Peck
Brand Luther	Andrew Pettegree
The Chosen, My Name is Asher Lev	Chaim Potok
Our Kids	Robert Putnam
The 5000 Year Leap	Cleon Skousen
Nature's Fortune	Adams, Tercek
The Outsiders	William Thorndike, Jr.
How Children Succeed	Paul Tough

[a] *The Clockwork Universe,* Edward Dolnick

[b] *Einstein,* Walter Isaacson

[c] By Allison & Blackwill

[d] By Jack & Suzy Welch

Concepts, Perspectives, and Practices

Book I: Toward Truth, Freedom, Fitness, and Decency

Losing Our Way
Inclusion Failures
The Change in the Election of U.S. Senators
Presidential Constitutional Failings
Supreme Court Constitutional Failings
Special Interest Government
Less Faith-Community Relevance
Less Integrity, Responsibility, and Civility
Promiscuity and the Decline of Marriage
Poorly Parented Children
Unionization of Education
Liberalization of Education
Social Justice Missteps
Relativism, Nonjudgmentalism, and Multiculturalism
Declining Discipline, Poor Habits, and Less Learning
Oligopoly and Monopoly
Offshoring
Entitlement
Consumerism and Debt
Easy Money
Hubris and Nation-Building
Immigration Failures
Distorted News
Political Polarization
Separation from Nature

Winning Perspectives
Singapore, Switzerland, and the United States
Country Characteristics
Winning Perspectives

Truth

Causality
Fallacy, Correlation, Necessity, and Sufficiency
The Inanimate and Animate Worlds

Scale

Evolution
Competition
Comparative Advantage
Natural Selection

Gradualism
Interrelated
Nature's Way

Fitness
Meritocracy
Procreation
The Underlying Aim of Life

Human Nature
Individual
Familial
Social
Super-organisms
Environmental Alignment

Periodic Disaster

Eco-Dependency
Externality

Winning Perspective Summary

Seven Levels of Winning Practices
Government, Enterprise,
Family, Education
Individual, Group
Culture
The Path of Fitness
Cultural Relativism
Winning Practices
Best Practices

Toward Truth, Freedom, Fitness, and Decency
Truth
Freedom
Fitness
Decency

Book II: Winning Practices of Government and Enterprise

Consumer-Driven Healthcare
Advantageous Immigration and Judicious Litigation
Goldilocks Minimum Wages and Savings Accounts
Universal Coverage
Patient Choice
Out-of-Pocket Payments

Assimilation
From Many, One
United We Stand, Divided We Fall
English as the National Language
Impervious Borders
Advantageous Immigration

Peace Through Fitness
Seven Levels of Human Fitness
Financial Strength
Law Enforcement and Justice
Military, Cyber, Intelligence Strength, and Restraint
Allies
Limited Treaty Powers
Democratic Realism

Sustainability
Fresh Water, Air, Land, and Ocean Quality
Ecosystem and Biodiversity Conservation
Resource Use, Recycling, and Waste Disposal
Clean Energy
Prudent Growth

A Final Note on Winning Practices of Government

Free Enterprise and Markets
Private Property
Free Enterprise
Public Goods
Profit
Free Markets
Free Trade
Comparative Advantage
Capital Formation and Investment

Responsible Corporate Governance
Stakeholder Inclusion
Independant and Stakeholder Directors
Media Reports of Corporate Misconduct
Winning Cultures

Prudent Regulation
Contract Enforcement
Transparency
Market Share Restrictions
Leverage Restrictions
Externality Taxation
Do No Harm
Long-Term Incentives

Enterprise Competitiveness
Customer Focus
A Performance and Improvement Culture
Minimal Overhead
Limited Leverage
Willing and Able Workforce
Well Developed Public Infrastructure
Minimal Government Burdens

Winning Culture
Looking Within and Without
Individual, Familial, Country, and Generational Minded
Winning Culture and The Path of Fitness
Prevalence of Winning Perspectives and Practices
Circle of Influence
Leadership and Service
Winning Culture

Book III: Winning Practices of Family and Education

Book IV: Winning Practices of Individuals and Groups

Winning Perspectives
Singapore, Switzerland, and the United States
Country Characteristics
Winning Perspectives

Seven Levels of Winning Practices
Government, Enterprise,
Family, Education
Individual, Group
Culture
The Path of Fitness
Cultural Relativism

Health and Renewal
Hygiene
Nutrition
Periodic Fasting
Sleep
Exercise
Avoiding Harm
Medical and Dental Care
DNA Fidelity
Reflection
Purpose and Sociability
Balance

Thought
Assimilation
Visualization
Creativity
Reverse Engineering
Research
Choice and Alignment
Focus
Rehearsal
Mentors

Priorities and Integrity
Awareness
Selection
The Effects Test
Scheduling and Review
Health, Family, Work, Community, Country
Truthfulness
Honorableness
Reliability

Proactivity
Responsibility
Constructive Speech and Action
Empowering Habit Formation
Purpose
Preparation
Work
Fitness Oriented Service

Excellence
Extra Thought, Focus, Effort, and Time
Standards, Improvement, Attention to Detail
Perseverance
Facilitators and Impediments

Thrift and Investment
Minimizing Expenditures
Automated Savings
Financial Tools and Investments
Rule of 69
Present Value and Future Value
Present and Future Value of an Annuity
Investment
Advantageously Buying and Selling Assets
Minimizing Taxes
The Keys to Wealth

Endnotes

1. Niall Ferguson, *Civilization: The West and the Rest*, The Penguin Press, New York, 2011, 5.

2. Alexander Hamilton, James Madison, and John Jay, *The Federalist Papers*, No. 45, Edited by Clinton Rossiter, Signet Classics, New York, 2003, 289.

3. "Obama Encourages Illegals," *The Washington Times*, Washington, D.C., November, 18, 2009, http://www.washingtontimes.com/news/2009/nov/18 /obama-encourages-illegals/.

4. Brion McClanahan, *9 Presidents Who Screwed Up America*, Regnery History, Washington, DC, 2016, 274.

5. James Madison, Speech at the Virginia Convention to Ratify the Federal Constitution, June 6, 1788, *Debates in the Several State Conventions on the Adoption of the Federal Constitution*, Jonathan Elliot, ed., Philadelphia, 1836, v.3, p. 87.

6. James Madison, "Letter to James Robertson," April 20, 1831, https:// en.wikisource.org/wiki/James_Madison_letter_to_James_Robertson.

7. Carol Tucker, "The 1950s–Powerful Years for Religion," USC News, June 16, 1997, https://news.usc.edu/25835/The-1950s-Powerful-Years-for-Religion/ and Shattuck, Kelly, "7 Startling Facts: An Up Close Look at Church Attendance in America," Church Leaders, Articles for Pastors, November, 2015, http://www .churchleaders.com/pastors/pastor-articles/139575-7-startling-facts-an-up-close -look-at-church-attendance-in-america.html.

8. National Institute of Alcohol Abuse and Alcoholism, http://www.niaaa.nih.gov /alcohol-health/overview-alcohol-consumption/alcohol-facts-and-statistics.

9. National Institute on Drug Abuse, http://www.drug abuse.gov/national/-survey -drug-use-health.

10. Karen Frazier, "Gambling Addition Statistics," http://addiction.lovetoknow.com .wiki/Gambling_Addiction_Statistics.

11. American Sexual Health Association, "Statistics," http://www.ashasexualhealth .org/stdsstis/statistics/.

12. American Safety Council, SafeMotorist.com, "Aggressive Driving and Road Rage," http://www.safemotorist.com/articles/road_rage.aspx.

13. NUMBEO, Crime Index for Country, 2015 Mid-Year, http://www.numbeo.com /crime/rankings_by_country.jsp.

14. Transparency International, 2014, https://www.transparency.org/cpi2014/results.

15. Cruz, Julissa, "Marriage: More than a Century of Change," Bowling Green State University, Bowling Green, OH, 2013, https://www.bgsu.edu/content/dam/BGSU /college-of-arts-and-sciences/NCFMR/documents/FP/FP-13-13.pdf.

16. Robert Putnam, Our Kids, Simon & Schuster, New York, 2015: 62-63.

17. Robert Putnam: 69–70.

18. Robert Putnam: 78–79.

19. David Brooks, "The Cost of Relativism," *The International New York Times,* March 11, 2015, 8.

20. Lee Kuan Yew, *Lee Kuan Yew: The Grand Master's Insights on China, The United States, and the World,* Graham Alison and Robert D. Blackwill, The MIT Press, Cambridge, 2013, 34.

21. U.S. Federal Reserve, Outstanding Debt by Sector, www.federalreserve.gov.

22. U.S. Bureau of Labor Statistics, Employment, www.bis.gov.

23. Pew Research Center, http://www.pewhispanic.org/2015/09/28/modern -immigration-wave-brings-59-million-to-u-s-driving-population-growth-and -change-through-2065/.

24. Central Intelligence Agency of the United States, *The World Fact Book*, 2015 https://www.cia.gov/library/publications/the-world-factbook.

25. Cato Institute, *The Human Freedom Index*, 2015, http://www.cato.org/human -freedom-index and "Economic Freedom of the World Rank," 2013, http://www.cato.org/economic-freedom-world/map.

26. Central Intelligence Agency of the United States, *The World Fact Book*, 2016 https://www.cia.gov/library/publications/the-world-factbook.

27. Wikipedia, "List of Countries by Home Ownership Rate," 2013–14, https://en.wikipedia.org/wiki/List_of_countries_by_home_ownership_rate.

28. Transparency International, 2014, https://www.transparency.org/cpi2014/results.

29. World Bank Economic Indicators, 2012.

30. Wikipedia, "List by Countries," 2013, https://en.wikipedia.org/wiki/List_of _countries_by_incarceration_rate.

31. Calculated using data from the Central Intelligence Agency of the United States, *The World Fact Book*, 2015, https://www.cia.gov/library/publications/the-world -factbook and International Monetary Fund, 2015, https://www.imf.org/external /np/sta/ir/IRProcessWeb/data/sgp/eng/cursgp.htm; International Monetary Fund, 2015, https://www.imf.org/external/np/sta/ir/IRProcessWeb/data/che/eng/curche .htm; International Monetary Fund, 2015, http://www.imf.org/external/np/sta/ir /IRProcessWeb/data/usa/eng/curusa.htm#I.

32. World Bank Economic Indicators, 2012.

33. Wikipedia, "Divorce Demography," https://en.wikipedia.org/wiki/Divorce _demography.

34. Populations decrease in size when fertility rates are below 2.1, World Bank Economic Indicators, 2014, http://databank.worldbank.org/data/reports .aspx?source=world-development-indicators#.

35. World Bank Economic Indicators, 2014.

36. Central Intelligence Agency of the United States, *The World Fact Book*, 2008, https://www.cia.gov/library/publications/the-world-factbook/rankorder/2228 rank.html.

37. Wikipedia, 2015, "Universal Health Coverage by Country," https://en.wikipedia
.org/wiki/Universal_health_coverage_by_country.

38. World Bank Economic Indicators, 2012.

39. World Bank Economic Indicators, 2012.

40. OECD, "Education at a Glance," 2014, http://www.oecd.org/edu/Education-at
-a-Glance-2014.pdf.

41. Wikipedia, "Education in Singapore," 2012, https://en.wikipedia.org/wiki
/Education_in_Singapore and "Researcher's Report 2014 Country Profile:
Switzerland," Deloitte, 4, http://ec.europa.eu/euraxess/pdf/research_policies
/country_files/Switzerland_Country_Profile_RR2014_FINAL.pdf.

42. World Bank Economic Indicators, 2014.

43. Central Intelligence Agency of the United States, *The World Fact Book*, 2016
https://www.cia.gov/library/publications/the-world-factbook.

44. World Bank Economic Indicators, 1960, Central Intelligence Agency of the
United States, *The World Fact Book*, 2016 https://www.cia.gov/library
/publications/the-world-factbook.

45. World Bank Economic Indicators, 2010.

46. World Bank Economic Indicators, 2010.

47. *Encyclopedia.com*, Jack Welch, http://www.encyclopedia.com/topic/Jack
_Welch.aspx.

48. Jack Welch, *Jack Straight from the Gut*, Warner Books, New York, 2001, 4.

49. Winston Churchill, Speech in the House of Commons, *Royal Assent*,
HC Deb 17 May, 1916, v. 82, cc 1578.

50. Dale Carnegie, *How to Stop Worrying and Start Living*, "Thomas Edison,"
Pocket Books, Kindle eBook, August 24, 2010, 36.

51. Carl Sagan, "Wonder and Skepticism," *Skeptical Enquirer*, Volume 19.1, January/
February 1995.

52. Carl Sagan, *The Demon-Haunted World: Science as a Candle in the Dark*,
Ballantine Books, New York, 1996, 28.

53. Will Durant, *The Story of Civilization, Volume 1: Our Oriental Heritage*,
Simon and Schuster, New York, 1954: 263–264.

54. Annie Dillard, *Pilgrim at Tinker Creek*, Bantam Books, Inc., New York, 1975: 9–10.

55. Charles Darwin, *On the Origin of Species*, 1859, 61.

56. Wikipedia, "Early Conditions," http://en.wikpedia.org/wiki/Abiogenesis.

57. Wikipedia, "Early Conditions."

58. Wikipedia, "Early Conditions."

59. Wikipedia, "Timeline of the Evolutionary History of Life," http://en.wikipedia.org
/wiki/Timeline_of_evolutionary_history_of_life.

60. Wikipedia, "Evolution," http://en.wikipedia.org/wiki/Evolution.

61. Wikipedia, "Evolution."

62. Wikipedia, "Evolution."

63. Wikipedia, "Evolution."

64. Wikipedia, "Timeline of the Evolutionary History of Life," http://en.wikpedia.org /wiki/Timeline_of_evolutionary_history_of_life.

65. Wikipedia, "Evolution," http://en.wikipedia.org/wiki/Evolution.

66. Wikipedia, "Timeline of the Evolutionary History of Life," http://en.wikpedia.org /wiki/Timeline_of_evolutionary_history_of_life.

67. Wikipedia, "Timeline of the Evolutionary History of Life."

68. Charles Darwin, *On the Origin of Species,* 1859, 61.

69. Wikipedia, "Origin of the Domestic Dog," https://en.wikipedia.org/wiki /Origin_of_the_domestic_dog.

70. E.O. Wilson *On Human Nature,* Harvard University Press, Cambridge, 1978, 88.

71. Will Durant, "The Map of Human Character," Lecture broadcast over WGN, Chicago, November 18, 1945, http://www.theimaginativeconservative .org/2012/05/map-of-human-character.html.

72. Wikipedia, "Total Fertility Rate of the United States," http://en.wikipedia.org /wiki/Total_fertility_rate, "United States."

73. Jared Diamond, *Guns, Germs, and Steel,* W.W. Norton, New York, Kindle eBook, April 17, 1999, 429.

74. Thomas Jefferson, "The Declaration of Independence of the United States of America," *The Declaration of Independence and the Constitutions of the United States of America,* Cato Institute, Washington, D. C., 9–10.

75. E.O. Wilson, *On Human Nature,* Harvard University Press, Cambridge, 1978, 84.

76. Robert Wright, *The Moral Animal: Why We Are the Way We Are: The New Science of Evolutionary Psychology,* Vintage Books, New York, 1995, 13.

77. E.O. Wilson, *On Human Nature,* Harvard University Press, Cambridge, 1978, 84.

78. David Brooks, "Social Animal: How the New Sciences of Human Nature Can Help Make Sense of Life," *Annals of Psychology,* January 17, 2011.

79. Wikipedia, "Extinction Events," http://en.wikipedia.org/wiki/Extinction_event.

80. Wikipedia, "World Population," http://en.wikipedia.org/wiki/World_population.

81. Wikipedia, "List of Famines," http://en.wikipedia.org/wiki/List_of_famines.

82. Wikipedia, "List of Famines."

83. Carl Sagan, *Pale Blue Dot: A Vision of the Human Future in Space,* Random House, New York, 1994, 371.

84. Nuclear Energy Institute, http://www.nei.org/Knowledge-Center /Nuclear-Statistics/On-Site-Storage-of-Nuclear-Waste.

85. E.O. Wilson, *Gaia Atlas of Planet Management* by Norman Myers, Anchor, Hamburg, 1992, 159.

86. David Biello, "How Much Is Too Much? Estimating Greenhouse Gas Emissions," *Scientific American,* April 2009.

87. Carl Sagan, *Cosmos: A Personal Voyage,* 1980, Episode 6, 58 min, 56 sec.

88. Geert Hofstede, Gert Jan Hofstede, and Michael Minkov, *Cultures and Organizations: Software of the Mind,* McGraw Hill, 2010: 3–12.

89. Geert Hofstede, Gert Jan Hofstede, and Michael Minkov: 12–14.

90. Geert Hofstede, Gert Jan Hofstede, and Michael Minkov: 53–88.

91. Charles Darwin, "Chapter V: On the Development of the Intellectual and Moral Faculties During Primeval and Civilized Times," *The Descent of Man,* 1871, 132, https://en.wikisource.org/wiki/The_Descent_of_Man_(Darwin)/Chapter_V.

92. Helen Keller, "Dreams That Come True," *Personality*, American Foundation for the Blind, December 1927.

93. Robert Levy and William Mellor, *The Dirty Dozen: How Twelve Supreme Court Cases Radically Expanded Government and Eroded Freedom*, Cato Institute, Washington, D. C., 2008: 50–66.

94. Levy and Mellor: 19–36.

95. Levy and Mellor: 181–197.

96. Levy and Mellor: 20–49.

97. Levy and Mellor: 67–85.

98. Levy and Mellor: 143–154.

99. Levy and Mellor: 67–85.

100. Levy and Mellor: 198–214.

101. Levy and Mellor: 155–168.

Index

An *f* following a page number indicates a figure on that page.

About the Author

Mark Bitz is a successful entrepreneur, author, and community leader. Unusually close to nature, well read and traveled, thoughtful, and pragmatic, he is a lifelong student of science, history, culture, government, economics, business, investing, and leadership.

Working his way up from farmhand to President, Mr. Bitz owned and operated Plainville Turkey Farm, Inc. between 1991 and 2007. Under his leadership, the company grew sevenfold and pioneered an all-natural-ingredient deli line, animal-friendly husbandry practices, turkeys grown without antibiotics, and turkeys raised on a vegetarian diet. The company won the American Culinary Institute Best Taste Award, and it was the first turkey company to receive the American Humane Association's "Free Farmed" certification. In 1990, he founded a feed company that he currently owns and operates, and in 2005, he cofounded CNY Crops, Inc., a company that became the largest organic crop operation in the Northeast.

Mr. Bitz has coached youth soccer and basketball. He was instrumental in the building of the Northwest YMCA in Baldwinsville, New York, and has served on numerous boards. He has chaired the Empire State Young President's Organization, Baldwinsville YMCA, and New York State 4-H Foundation. He has been a director of the Greater Syracuse YMCA, Syracuse Metropolitan Development Association, New York State Business Council, National Turkey Federation, and International Chief Executives Organization. He served on the Cornell Agriculture and Life Science Dean's Advisory Board and the Cornell University Council. Currently, he is a trustee of the Florida Nature Conservancy and Vice President of Education of the Chief Executives Organization.

Mr. Bitz received his B.S. in Economic Development from Purdue University. He was a recipient of the Lehman Fellowship at Cornell where he received his MS in Agricultural Economics and completed the coursework and exams toward a PhD in Public Policy Analysis. He has attended numerous Harvard and Oxford Executive Programs. He was named among the "CNY 40 Under 40" and is the recipient of the Purdue University Alumni of Distinction Award. His turkey business was the Onondaga County Conservation Farm of the Year and the New York State Agricultural Society Business of the Year. He and his wife, Leokadia, have two sons, two daughters-in-law, and a granddaughter.